Deadly Viruses

Other Books in the Current Controversies Series

Deadly Viruses

Noah Berlatsky, Book Editor

GREENHAVEN PRESS
A part of Gale, Cengage Learning

Farmington Hills, Mich • San Francisco • New York • Waterville, Maine
Meriden, Conn • Mason, Ohio • Chicago

Judy Galens, *Manager, Frontlist Acquisitions*

© 2016 Greenhaven Press, a part of Gale, Cengage Learning

Gale and Greenhaven Press are registered trademarks used herein under license.

For more information, contact:
Greenhaven Press
27500 Drake Rd.
Farmington Hills, MI 48331-3535
Or you can visit our Internet site at gale.cengage.com

For product information and technology assistance, contact us at

Gale Customer Support, 1-800-877-4253
For permission to use material from this text or product, submit all requests online at www.cengage.com/permissions

Further permissions questions can be emailed to permissionrequest@cengage.com

Articles in Greenhaven Press anthologies are often edited for length to meet page requirements. In addition, original titles of these works are changed to clearly present the main thesis and to explicitly indicate the author's opinion. Every effort is made to ensure that Greenhaven Press accurately reflects the original intent of the authors. Every effort has been made to trace the owners of copyrighted material.

Cover image © Festa/Shutterstock.com.

LIBRARY OF CONGRESS CATALOGING-IN-PUBLICATION DATA

Deadly viruses / Noah Berlatsky, book editor.
     pages cm. -- (Current controversies)
     Includes bibliographical references and index.
     978-0-7377-7428-3 (hardcover) -- ISBN 978-0-7377-7429-0 (pbk.)
     1. Communicable diseases--Treatment. I. Berlatsky, Noah, editor.
     RC111.D38 2016
     616.9--dc23
                                                                   2015024204

Printed in Mexico
1 2 3 4 5 6 7 19 18 17 16 15

Contents

Michael Gerson

Ebola is still a serious threat to West Africa and to the world. Despite claims that Ebola has been contained, there is still no vaccine. Ebola requires major behavioral changes among populations to keep it from spreading, since infected people and dead bodies must be quarantined. As long as that is the case, more vigorous educational and health efforts are needed. The American government needs to devote more resources to crafting an innovative and serious policy for Ebola.

Gregory Korte

President Barack Obama has taken unprecedented steps to involve the military in containing the outbreak of Ebola. These steps are necessary and have gained bipartisan support. However, more aid is needed from other countries if the spread of Ebola is to be prevented.

*Luis Fábregas, Adam Smeltz, and
Megha Satyanarayana*

Ebola is an extremely deadly disease and American health officials and systems do not seem to be prepared to deal with it adequately. When a case of Ebola did appear in the United States, health authorities were slow to react and failed to contain it properly. The Centers for Disease Control and Prevention has also arguably downplayed the infectiousness of the virus in order to prevent public panic. The US government and health system needs to move forward quickly with plans for dealing with more Ebola cases throughout the country.

The response to Ebola has been inadequate. The global health-care system particularly failed in identifying early cases of the virus, allowing it to spread out of control. However, there have been successes in early containment efforts. These must be built upon; the United States needs to invest money in developing a vaccine, and the world needs to create better systems to track contagious viruses early.

No: Ebola Is Not a Serious Threat

Scientists are unlikely to create an effective vaccine against Ebola in the near future. Vaccines take time and money to develop. There has previously been little interest in an Ebola vaccine because over the last few decades, the virus has resulted in few casualties. In addition, Ebola has been most deadly in West Africa, a region of the world with few resources to pay for viral research. The recent high-profile cases of Ebola will probably create a surge in funding and money. Eventually, it seems likely that a vaccine will be developed, though the process will be slow.

The United States and many other nations have responded to the Ebola threat by treating it as a security issue. In other words, it is presented to the public as an existential danger that must be handled by extraordinary means, such as by military and security forces. This causes public panic, which can be costly and dangerous. It also empowers military forces, which can erode civil liberties. It would be better to see disease prevention in general as a public good and set up international funds to confront it, rather than treating the advent of each disease as a major crisis. This is especially true since Ebola has virtually no chance of creating a serious public health emergency in the United States.

Anna C. Dragsbaek

Ebola is a frightening disease because of the difficulty of treatment. But it poses no serious danger in Texas, where the health-care system is well-equipped to prevent its spread and treat victims. However, Texas is threatened by a number of communicable diseases, including influenza and pertussis. Parents who refuse to immunize their children are also a threat, and dropping rates of immunization may allow diseases like measles to regain a foothold. Rather than focusing on Ebola, therefore, Texas needs to focus on actual dangerous diseases, and on increasing immunization rates.

World Health Organization

There is currently no Ebola vaccine available, but many vaccines are being developed and proceeding through clinical trials. There are several medicines and drug therapies that can be used against Ebola. There are also diagnostic tests for Ebola, though these can be challenging to conduct in areas far from hospitals or under outbreak conditions. In such instances, the World Health Organization recommends the establishment of mobile laboratories.

Chapter 2: Should Vaccines Against Deadly Viruses Be Compulsory?

Some parents believe that vaccines cause autism and other harmful effects and therefore refuse to vaccinate their children. The link between vaccines and autism has been completely debunked; danger from diseases are exponentially higher than danger from vaccine reactions, which are very rare. Showing anti-vaxxers the science should in theory cause them to be willing to vaccinate. However, a study showed that anti-vaxxers provided with evidence disproving their beliefs actually became more resistant to vaccination, not less. Since explanation does little good, tightening restrictions on exemptions, or other mildly coercive measures, seem like the best way to increase vaccination rates.

Edith N. Nyangoma et al.

Foreign children adopted by parents in the United States are supposed to receive vaccinations. In some cases, these vaccination requirements are waived until they arrive in the United States. This can result in diseases like measles being brought into the country from overseas, as was the case with two nonimmunized children from China in 2013. The government should ensure that all adopted children are vaccinated before traveling to the United States. The government should also adopt stricter standards for testing children for diseases like measles before they come to the United States.

No: Vaccines Against Deadly Viruses Should Not Be Compulsory

Jeffrey A. Singer

There is no way to prove that someone who is not vaccinated will become infected with a disease, or will infect someone else. Punishing someone for a crime or harm they have not committed is intrusive and violent. Vaccinating someone against their will is an aggressive infringement on liberty and gives too much power to government. Instead, government and society should work to persuade individuals to vaccinate. This entails some risk, but some risk is inevitable—and necessary—in a free society.

News outlets, especially on the right, often claim that immigrants from Mexico and Latin America seriously threaten the United States with communicable diseases. This is false. Vaccine rates for children in much of Latin America are higher than those in the United States; the United States has had outbreaks of measles recently, while most nations in Latin America have not. Immigrant children also do not have high rates of tuberculosis (TB), and even if they did, the United States has adequate health resources to quickly contain any TB cases. The fears about immigrants carrying diseases are caused by antipathy toward immigrants. There is no real danger.

Chapter 3: Does an HIV/AIDS Crisis Still Exist?

Media often presents the AIDS epidemic in America as being over or winding down. However, rates of AIDS among African Americans remain proportionately high. African American communities often see AIDS as associated with gay white men. Because of this association, African Americans who contract AIDS often face homophobia and stigma and may be afraid to report the disease. In fact, though, the disease is more frequently found among heterosexuals than gays in the African American population. As long as myths about AIDS persist, it will be difficult to confront the disease and prevent its transmission within African American communities.

China has a serious problem with AIDS, caused in part by the government itself, which spread the disease through poorly conducted blood donor programs. Those infected are often stigmatized and shunned; they may be refused treatment in hospitals. The silence around AIDS makes it difficult to control the disease, encouraging people to hide their infection from partners and to spread the disease through sexual contact. The government has made some moves toward compensating victims, but the efforts have not really addressed the scale of the problem.

While AIDS infection rates are falling in some parts of the world, they are actually rising in Russia. This is in large part because of Russian government policy toward the disease. Russia stigmatizes the lesbian, gay, bisexual, and transgender (LGBT) community and has passed laws against discussing or distributing "propaganda" about homosexuality. This has created a climate of distrust in which people are afraid to discuss AIDS for fear they will be stigmatized as LGBT. Russia's official prejudice has prevented the dissemination of accurate information about AIDS and hindered other health-care efforts. Russia needs to end its official homophobia in order to confront the AIDS health crisis.

Africa continues to have a serious AIDS crisis. In southern Africa in particular, some countries have HIV infection rates approaching one-fifth or even a quarter of the population. Slow rates of economic growth, prejudice, and laws criminalizing transmission of AIDS are all factors that, in various countries, interfere with fighting the AIDS epidemic. International aid and domestic initiatives have helped to address the crisis, but AIDS will continue to be a major health, social, and economic problem in Africa for some time to come.

The discovery of two people exposed to the AIDS virus who did not develop the disease has caused speculation about a possible AIDS cure. However, there is no reason to think an AIDS cure is imminent. The rush to declare a possible cure simply raises the hopes of AIDS sufferers, only to dash them. It is irresponsible for news organizations to encourage unrealistic expectations of AIDS cures in the near future.

No: An HIV/AIDS Crisis Does Not Exist

AIDS is still a heavy burden in South Africa, especially among those trying to raise and care for the children of those who have died. In the early 2000s, it seemed likely that South Africa's population would be decimated by AIDS. Since then, however, antiretroviral (ARV) therapies and increased understanding of the virus have drastically reduced infection rates. ARV has also made AIDS a disease that people can live with for many years, rather than a certain and swift death sentence.

In the early 1990s, Australia's gay community was devastated by the AIDS virus. Activists fought hard for the government to provide services and recognize the crisis. They also quasi-legally imported early antiretroviral drugs, since official drug approval was slow and ignored the scale of the disease. As better treatments became available, and AIDS ceased to be a death sentence, many activists moved back to their regular lives. Today, most activists agree the AIDS crisis in Australia is over, though it continues in other parts of the world.

At one time, researchers were afraid to even mention a possible cure for AIDS, because they did not want to raise false hopes. Now, however, it seems like a real possibility that a cure might be feasible. Two people have apparently been cured of the disease by different, complicated methods, and though their cures are not reproducible, they may help scientists to develop treatments that could help more individuals. Finding a cure is important as well because AIDS may mutate and adapt to defeat the antiretroviral drugs that control it, and because AIDS continues to be a major killer worldwide.

Chapter 4: What Are Other Controversies About Deadly Viruses?

The smallpox virus is almost completely eliminated; it only officially exists in two laboratories. The World Health Organization believes the last samples in labs should be destroyed, rendering the virus extinct. However, there is no guarantee that some smallpox sample does not survive elsewhere. That means that there is potential for another smallpox outbreak. Given the deadliness of the smallpox virus, the samples that remain in labs should be preserved for study, and to make sure doctors and researchers are prepared to deal with a possible outbreak.

The remaining smallpox virus samples in two secure locations have been of little use to researchers and have added nothing to scientific knowledge for many years. The chance that the virus could be released from its secure locations is small, but it does exist. If smallpox were to be released, it could still do terrible harm. But the smallpox samples themselves would be of little use in an outbreak, since they are not needed to make a vaccine. Weighing benefits and risks, the smallpox virus samples should be eliminated.

Foreword

By definition, controversies are "discussions of questions in which opposing opinions clash" (*Webster's Twentieth Century Dictionary Unabridged*). Few would deny that controversies are a pervasive part of the human condition and exist on virtually every level of human enterprise. Controversies transpire between individuals and among groups, within nations and between nations. Controversies supply the grist necessary for progress by providing challenges and challengers to the status quo. They also create atmospheres where strife and warfare can flourish. A world without controversies would be a peaceful world; but it also would be, by and large, static and prosaic.

The Series' Purpose

The purpose of the Current Controversies series is to explore many of the social, political, and economic controversies dominating the national and international scenes today. Titles selected for inclusion in the series are highly focused and specific. For example, from the larger category of criminal justice, Current Controversies deals with specific topics such as police brutality, gun control, white collar crime, and others. The debates in Current Controversies also are presented in a useful, timeless fashion. Articles and book excerpts included in each title are selected if they contribute valuable, long-range ideas to the overall debate. And wherever possible, current information is enhanced with historical documents and other relevant materials. Thus, while individual titles are current in focus, every effort is made to ensure that they will not become quickly outdated. Books in the Current Controversies series will remain important resources for librarians, teachers, and students for many years.

In addition to keeping the titles focused and specific, great care is taken in the editorial format of each book in the series. Book introductions and chapter prefaces are offered to provide background material for readers. Chapters are organized around several key questions that are answered with diverse opinions representing all points on the political spectrum. Materials in each chapter include opinions in which authors clearly disagree as well as alternative opinions in which authors may agree on a broader issue but disagree on the possible solutions. In this way, the content of each volume in Current Controversies mirrors the mosaic of opinions encountered in society. Readers will quickly realize that there are many viable answers to these complex issues. By questioning each author's conclusions, students and casual readers can begin to develop the critical thinking skills so important to evaluating opinionated material.

Current Controversies is also ideal for controlled research. Each anthology in the series is composed of primary sources taken from a wide gamut of informational categories including periodicals, newspapers, books, US and foreign government documents, and the publications of private and public organizations. Readers will find factual support for reports, debates, and research papers covering all areas of important issues. In addition, an annotated table of contents, an index, a book and periodical bibliography, and a list of organizations to contact are included in each book to expedite further research.

Perhaps more than ever before in history, people are confronted with diverse and contradictory information. During the Persian Gulf War, for example, the public was not only treated to minute-to-minute coverage of the war, it was also inundated with critiques of the coverage and countless analyses of the factors motivating US involvement. Being able to sort through the plethora of opinions accompanying today's major issues, and to draw one's own conclusions, can be a complicated and frustrating struggle. It is the editors' hope that Current Controversies will help readers with this struggle.

Introduction

> *"It is possible to contain rabies so that no humans die from it. We know this is possible because it has largely been accomplished in Western nations like the United States."*

Rabies is a viral infection that can be transmitted through animal bites. It causes tens of thousands of deaths a year, according to the World Health Organization. It would cause hundreds of thousands more, but there is a vaccine that can be administered post-bite and prevents the disease.[1] As it is, poorer regions of the world suffer the most from rabies deaths, most of them (99 percent) inflicted by dog bites. Asia accounts for 60 percent of deaths, and Africa for 36 percent. India, with 35 percent of rabies deaths, has the most rabies deaths of any country in the world.

Victims need to receive the rabies vaccine quickly, usually within a day, and take other doses over a month. The complexity of the vaccine regime makes rabies shots expensive and difficult, especially for those in poor regions of the world; it is estimated that rabies costs around $583 million a year.

Death from rabies is particularly horrible. If not vaccinated, the rabies virus attacks the brain. The first symptoms are similar to those of the flu, including general weakness, fever, or headache, progressing within days to more serious symptoms, such as cerebral dysfunction, agitation, delirium, hallucinations, and insomnia. This advanced stage also often includes a fear of water and inability to consume liquids by

---

1. World Health Organization, "Rabies" Fact Sheet No. 99, September 2014. http://www.who.int/mediacentre/factsheets/fs099/en.

the patient, known as hydrophobia. Eventually, these symptoms give way to paralysis and death.

Given the deadliness of rabies, and given the fact that there is a vaccine that works against it, many commentators have argued that the disease should be eliminated. For example, Louis Nel, executive director of the Global Alliance for Rabies Control, told BBC News that "no one should die of rabies and we will continue to work together towards global rabies elimination."[2]

Nel is not arguing that rabies should be wiped out, as smallpox has been. That is probably impossible, because animals, as well as humans, can contract the disease. Inoculating wild animals like raccoons and bats is simply not feasible. Thus, rabies will probably never be eradicated entirely, as smallpox has been.

However, it is possible to contain rabies so that no humans die from it. We know this is possible because it has largely been accomplished in Western nations like the United States. Nel's comments were in part based on the fact that deaths from rabies have been almost entirely eliminated in Western countries. This has been accomplished through the widespread vaccination of domestic dogs. Once domesticated dogs are protected, humans are as well.

Such a vaccination regime could be undertaken in other nations too, Olivia Judson suggests at *The New York Times*. "In principle—if we were super-organized—we could do this with one huge and coordinated dog vaccination campaign. More realistically, however, a concerted effort would take four or five years to do the job," Judson argues. She adds, "so many of the problems we face are huge and hard to solve—climate change, malaria, war in the Middle East, destruction of the

2. BBC News, "Preventable Rabies Kills 160 People Per Day," April 17, 2015. http://www.bbc.com/news/health-32336099.

rain forests. Rabies is not on that list. To deal with it is just a matter of logistics and money. We should act. Now."[3]

So if it should be done, why hasn't it? Virginia Hughes, writing at *National Geographic*, explains that the problem is mostly bureaucratic. In Asia, Africa, and India, veterinary budgets are usually kept separate from human health budgets. Veterinary attention is focused mostly on preserving livestock and preventing economic damage from diseases that affect cows, sheep, chickens, and other animals. Rabid dogs seldom pass on their disease to livestock; therefore, veterinary efforts rarely focus on rabies. As a result, cattle are protected—but people die.

Countries in Latin and South America have managed to overcome similar hurdles and institute effective anti-rabies programs. Other nations have taken steps in this direction as well; Kenya, for instance, has organized a long-term effort to vaccinate dogs led by veterinarians and human health officials. Tanzania also has had a successful program; the country vaccinated 70 percent of dogs, reducing rabies cases from fifty a year to zero. As this suggests, vaccination does not even need to be 100 percent to protect humans; the disease travels slowly enough between dogs that 70 percent vaccination rates can eliminate all human cases. Rabies should not be that difficult a disease to eliminate. But as with other viral diseases, implementing the right public policy can be a struggle.

The remainder of this book looks at other current controversies around deadly viruses in such chapters as "Is Ebola a Serious Threat?," "Should Vaccines Against Deadly Viruses Be Compulsory?," "Does an HIV/AIDS Crisis Still Exist?," and "What Are Other Controversies About Deadly Viruses?" Each chapter also addresses concerns covered in this introduction,

3. Olivia Judson, "A Coffin for Rabies," *New York Times*, January 15, 2008. http://opinionator.blogs.nytimes.com/2008/01/15/a-coffin-for-rabies/?_r=1.

such as how viruses can be contained; what role vaccines can play; and how, and to what extent, deadly viruses can be eliminated.

CHAPTER 1

Is Ebola a Serious Threat?

Chapter Preface

The 2014 outbreak of the deadly Ebola virus was concentrated in West Africa, especially in the countries of Liberia, Guinea, and Sierra Leone. As of mid-April 2015, Sierra Leone had more than twelve thousand reported cases and more than 3,800 deaths.

Ebola's impact on the country goes well beyond the death toll, however. Sierra Leone is one of the poorest countries in the world, and has just started to recover from a lengthy and bitter civil war. Economists had thought that 2014 would be a year of fast and vital growth for Sierra Leone; because of Ebola, however, that growth never materialized.

Fear of the virus—and efforts to contain it—devastated the already struggling nation. People were afraid to associate with one another lest they expose themselves; as a result, economic activity ground to a halt. Iron ore mines, central to the economy, were closed; farmers ceased to work in their fields; and small businesses shuttered. According to President Ernest Bai Koroma, "Because of Ebola, most businesses shut down. A good number of the mining companies ceased operations, flights were canceled to the country, tourism was brought to a standstill. . . . Nobody ventured in, nobody will discuss business at this time."[1]

The virus took a brutal toll on the nation's health-care system as well. Sierra Leone only had 134 doctors for its six million people; eleven of them were killed by the disease. The government is trying to train new doctors and nurses, but more aid is desperately needed. Education too has been affected by the virus; schools that closed in September 2014 only reopened in mid-April 2015.

1. Quoted in Peter Clottey, "Sierra Leone President Bemoans Ebola's Impact," *Voice of America*, April 15, 2015. http://www.voanews.com/content/sierra-leone-president-koroma-bemoans-ebola-impact-on-economy/2720972.html.

Rebuilding after the virus is a long, difficult task. The virus as of mid-April still had not been entirely contained, as new cases continued to trickle in (the outbreak will only be considered over when there are no new cases for forty-two days). Reopening mines has been difficult because of the low price of iron. Tourists have not started to return. Still, with international aid, President Koroma has hopes that Sierra Leone can move again toward growth. "The country is opening up for business once more," he said. "It is beginning to look up."[2]

The rest of this chapter looks at controversies surrounding Ebola and how best to address the virus.

2. Quoted in Todd C. Frankel, "Ebola on the Wane, Sierra Leone Braces for a Whole New Crisis," *Washington Post*, April 16, 2015. http://www.washingtonpost.com/blogs /wonkblog/wp/2015/04/16/ebola-on-the-wane-sierra-leone-braces-for-a-whole-new -crisis.

The World Is in Denial About Ebola's True Threat

Michael Gerson

Michael Gerson is an op-ed columnist for the Washington Post *and a policy fellow with the ONE campaign.*

It is such a relief about that Ebola thing. The threat of a U.S. outbreak turned out to be overhyped. A military operation is underway to help those poor Liberians. An Ebola czar (what is his name again?) has been appointed to coordinate the U.S. government response. The growth of the disease in Africa, by some reports, seems to have slowed. On to the next crisis.

Out of Control

Except that this impression of control is an illusion, and a particularly dangerous one.

The Ebola virus has multiplied in a medium of denial. There was the initial denial that a rural disease, causing isolated outbreaks that burned out quickly, could become a sustained, urban killer. There is the (understandable) denial of patients in West Africa, who convince themselves that they have flu or malaria (the symptoms are similar to Ebola) and remain in communities. And there is the form of denial now practiced by Western governments—a misguided belief that an incremental response can get ahead of an exponentially growing threat.

The remarkable success of Nigerian authorities in tracing and defeating their Ebola outbreak has created a broad impression that the disease is contained. Some administration officials are privately citing the news of empty hospital beds in parts of Liberia as a welcome development.

But the disease is not contained within Liberia and Sierra Leone. Aid officials debate the reasons for empty beds in some health-care facilities. Are people infected with Ebola staying at home out of fear (since reporting to a health-care facility must seem like a death sentence)? Is this a dip in infections before the next rise—a phenomenon we've seen before? Are there many more invisible cases beyond the reach of roads and communications? (The relief organization Samaritan's Purse reports finding some remote villages in Liberia decimated by the disease.) The least likely explanation, at this point, is that Ebola has run its course.

Until there is a vaccine, limiting the spread of Ebola depends on education and behavior change. People must be persuaded to do things that violate powerful human inclinations. A parent must be persuaded not to touch a sick child. A relative must be persuaded not to respectfully prepare a body for burial. A man or woman with a fever must be persuaded to prepare for the worst instead of hoping for the best. This is the exceptional cruelty of Ebola—it requires human beings to overcome humane instincts for comfort, tradition and optimism. And this difficult education must come from trusted sources in post-conflict societies where few institutions have established public trust.

Few aid officials believe Liberia or Sierra Leone are prepared for the coming wave.

The Ebola virus has sometimes been like a fire in a pine forest—burning in hidden ways along the floor before suddenly flaring. There are, perhaps, 12,000 Ebola cases in West Africa. The World Health Organization warns there may be 5,000 to 10,000 new cases each week by December [2014]. This would quickly overwhelm existing and planned health capacity (1,700 proposed beds in Liberia from the U.S. military, perhaps 1,000 beds in community care centers).

End Denial

At this level of infection, the questions become: Is Ebola containable? Will we see disease-related hunger? How will rice crops be harvested and transported? What effects will spiking food prices have on civil order? Might there be large-scale, disease-related migration? What would be the economic effects on all of Africa? Many are still refusing to look at these (prospective) horrors full in the face.

This denial is reflected in the scale and urgency of the global response, including by the United States. Of the 3,000 troops promised by President [Barack] Obama in September, just a few hundred are now on the ground. The first U.S.-built hospital—a 25-bed facility for foreign health workers—will not open until early November. The airlift of supplies for aid groups within Liberia is still not functioning at scale. Some local capabilities (such as corpse removal) have improved. But few aid officials believe Liberia or Sierra Leone are prepared for the coming wave.

The appointment of Ron Klain as Ebola czar—commanding no immediate respect from either the military or the public health community—reveals a disposition. The White House believes it has a management and communications challenge. But the problem is far larger: the inability (so far) to get ahead of the crisis in West Africa with decisive action. This points to a useful role for Klain and other White House staffers—not to make the current Ebola policy process run smoothly but to blow it up in search of sufficient answers.

Obama Announces Military Response to Ebola

Gregory Korte

Gregory Korte is a White House correspondent for USA Today.

Facing an unprecedented and out-of-control Ebola epidemic in West Africa, President [Barack] Obama announced an equally unprecedented response Tuesday [September 2014]—dispatching 3,000 U.S. troops to the region with health care and aid workers in an effort to contain the deadly virus.

Large-Scale Response

The expanded, $763 million, military-led plan will include a new regional U.S. base in Liberia; portable hospitals, laboratories and other medical facilities; and increased training for first responders and other medical officials throughout West Africa.

It's the largest response to an international epidemic in U.S. history, Obama said after meeting with the nation's top public health officials at the Centers for Disease Control and Prevention [CDC] in Atlanta.

Will it be enough?

"There is no guarantee of success, but there would be a guarantee of failure if Obama hadn't announced this plan," said Daniel Lucey, an adjunct professor of microbiology and immunology at Georgetown University Medical Center.

"This is urban Ebola," said Lucey, a doctor who treated Ebola patients in Sierra Leone for three weeks in August. "It's unprecedented, and it's uncontrolled."

Obama acknowledged as much. "In West Africa, Ebola is now an epidemic of the likes that we have not seen before. It's spiraling out of control. It is getting worse. It's spreading faster and exponentially," he said.

The president said the solution is within grasp.

"The world knows how to fight this disease," Obama said. "It's not a mystery. We know the science. We know how to prevent it from spreading. We know how to care for those who contract it. We know that if we take the proper steps, we can save lives. But we have to act fast. We can't dawdle on this one."

Obama said Army Maj. Gen. Darryl Williams will lead the African effort. He's already arrived in Liberia, where he will set up a regional command center in the capital, Monrovia. His mission is to provide engineering and logistical help, establishing an "air bridge" into Africa to more quickly get medical supplies and aid workers to the continent.

More than 100 experts from the CDC are in Africa, where they will help train 500 new health workers every week.

"Some people have asked why the military should be involved," said Sen. Lamar Alexander, R-Tenn., at a Senate hearing. "They have to be involved if we want to deal with the problem. There's no way for the doctors and nurses and health care workers to deal with it" without such help, he said.

The mission, dubbed Operation United Assistance, is modeled after the U.S. response to the earthquake in Haiti in 2010, when 20,000 U.S. troops helped get aid into the country. U.S. troops will not provide "direct medical care," White House spokesman Josh Earnest said.

That will be the job of health care providers. More than 100 experts from the CDC are in Africa, where they will help train 500 new health workers every week.

"This new response, we think, is spot on for what's needed," said Bruce Johnson, president of SIM USA, a Christian missionary group that runs the ELWA Ebola treatment center in Monrovia. He said other nations must also step up. "Now we need about triple this from the rest of the world community to fight this wildfire of Ebola."

Infectious disease experts said the world is racing against time. Infections are doubling at the rate of about once every three weeks, and the longer Ebola rages out of control the more likely it could spread to other continents or—in a nightmare scenario—mutate to become airborne. The virus spreads only through direct contact with bodily fluids.

Nations Must Act Quickly

"The window of opportunity to contain this outbreak is closing," said Joanne Liu, president of Doctors Without Borders, at a United Nations briefing in Geneva on Tuesday. "We need more countries to stand up, we need greater deployment, and we need it now."

She said sick people are banging on the doors of the group's Ebola hospitals in Monrovia, desperate for a safe place where they won't spread the disease to their families. "Tragically, our teams must turn them away," she said.

The United States hopes to prevent people from contracting the [Ebola] virus in the first place, through better hygiene.

As of Tuesday, the World Health Organization reported 4,963 confirmed cases and 2,453 deaths in the hardest-hit nations of Liberia, Guinea and Sierra Leone.

If the virus keeps spreading at the current rate, "there simply aren't going to be enough beds," said Ken Isaacs of Samaritan's Purse, a missionary group that has run an Ebola treatment center in Monrovia.

His organization hopes to train people to treat family members with Ebola at home. "We ran Ebola treatment centers for two months, and we were totally overwhelmed," Isaacs said. "Isolating people in their homes and training the family members to protect themselves is the way we can influence disease transmission."

The United States hopes to prevent people from contracting the virus in the first place, through better hygiene.

Helped by $9 million from the Paul Allen Family Foundation, the U.S. Agency for International Development will provide 400,000 "household protection kits" to be distributed by local volunteers. The kit includes a bucket, refuse bags, cleaning supplies, four surgical gowns, 25 surgical masks, six bars of soap, 100 latex gloves, chlorine and an information leaflet.

Support for the president's Ebola direction enjoyed rare bipartisan support on Capitol Hill. "The president's absolutely right," said Senate Majority Leader Harry Reid, D-Nev. "And no one's better equipped to do something like this than our military."

Senate Minority Leader Mitch McConnell, R-Ky., announced his intention to support the funding bill that would include $88 million in additional Ebola funds. "What the administration is doing is correct," he said.

Ebola Threat in US, and We're Not Prepared to Contain It, Experts Warn

Luis Fábregas, Adam Smeltz, and Megha Satyanarayana

Luis Fábregas, Adam Smeltz, and Megha Satyanarayana are staff writers for Trib Total Media.

Mistakes and missteps in the handling of the first Ebola case in the United States trouble lawmakers, international organizations and some public health experts who say the government needs to step up its strategy to contain the virus.

"Where is the 1-800-Ebola hotline?" asked Gavin MacGregor-Skinner, an assistant professor of public health at Penn State University who helped set up an Ebola treatment clinic in Nigeria a few weeks ago. "This is a Category 5 hurricane. It just happens to be viral."

Doctors have diagnosed only one person with Ebola in the United States, but as many as 50 people might have been exposed to the virus in Dallas, according to the Centers for Disease Control and Prevention.

Doctors at Howard University Hospital in Washington are monitoring a patient with Ebola-like symptoms who frequently traveled to Nigeria.

The raging epidemic has overwhelmed weak health systems in the West African nations of Guinea, Liberia and Sierra Leone. Although hospitals in the United States are better prepared to handle Ebola, travel restrictions or stricter screening of people coming to the United States from Ebola-affected countries might be necessary to curb the crisis, some health monitors said.

"Unless the World Health Organization and the Centers for Disease Control and Prevention take extreme measures to prevent the universal spread of the disease, we could possibly end up with a pandemic," said Phenelle Segal, president of Montgomery County-based Infection Control Consulting Services and a former infection prevention analyst for the Pennsylvania Patient Safety Authority.

"I think as soon as we started seeing West Africa go out of control with Ebola, that was the time" to halt air travel from the region, said Segal, who supports exceptions for relief workers and aid missions.

That approach might be the only way to contain the outbreak and prevent a global crisis, Segal said. Federal and global health officials argue isolation would risk more economic instability in West Africa while undercutting humanitarian support, worsening the epidemic in the short term and fostering a greater international threat over time.

U.S. Rep Tim Murphy, R-Upper St. Clair, plans an Oct. 16 hearing with officials from the CDC, National Institutes of Health and others to examine whether tougher measures are needed to screen travelers.

Cases of Ebola have doubled every three weeks in West Africa, where the disease has killed more than 3,400 people.

"The propensity of people coming out of those countries may be to get out of there as fast as possible, even if that means lying on their records. We can't necessarily just use that verbal screening process," Murphy said. "CDC and NIH are going to tell us how they are adapting and changing this, because the current process apparently is not effective."

Sen. Jerry Moran, a Kansas Republican, urged President Obama to appoint someone to coordinate Ebola-related matters.

"This is a serious development and reiterates the need for us to heighten coordination and vigilance to address this health crisis," Moran said.

Virus Spreading Fast

Cases of Ebola have doubled every three weeks in West Africa, where the disease has killed more than 3,400 people.

The United States pledged $750 million in aid to West Africa, and the Pentagon said it could put as many as 4,000 troops in affected countries. The military would help build hospitals and a clinic for infected physicians and health care workers.

Great Britain plans facilities for 700 medical beds in Sierra Leone, and Japan promised $22 million in emergency aid for the region.

The Obama administration's response was not swift enough for organizations such as Doctors Without Borders, whose workers are on the front lines.

"The sick are desperate, their families and caregivers are angry, and aid workers are exhausted. Maintaining quality of care is an extreme challenge," Joanne Chiu, the organization's executive director, told the United Nations this month.

The Ebola outbreak shows no signs of abating. More than 7,000 people are infected in West Africa, where people often distrust the government and aid workers. The lack of a treatment for the virus has affected the ability of international aid groups to help people with the illness, which causes high fever, vomiting and diarrhea.

Since the identification of Thomas E. Duncan as the first person diagnosed with Ebola in the United States, errors have occurred in the attempt to contain the virus, experts said. Authorities accused Duncan of lying on a form in Liberia that asked whether he had contact with anyone with Ebola.

He fell ill on arrival in Dallas, but a hospital sent him home with antibiotics. When he was finally admitted, local officials stalled in identifying a cleaning crew to remove contaminated linens and furniture from the apartment where Duncan stayed.

Ebola kills up to 90 percent of those who get it, but CDC officials caution that it is not a respiratory virus and can be contracted only though direct contact with bodily fluids.

Even then, authorities turned away the crew because they did not have appropriate biohazard transportation permits.

MacGregor-Skinner cited poor communication between federal agencies—and with state and local agencies—on which hospitals are equipped to handle Ebola patients, how to safely contain and transport people, and what to do with contaminated waste.

Tamping Down Panic

Ebola kills up to 90 percent of those who get it, but CDC officials caution that it is not a respiratory virus and can be contracted only though direct contact with bodily fluids.

"This is not like flu. It's not like measles. It's not like the common cold. It's not as spreadable. It's not as infectious. What's scary is that it is so severe if you get infected," said Dr. Thomas Frieden, the CDC's director.

Yet the CDC appears to be avoiding hysteria by downplaying how easily the disease can spread, including through sweat, said Segal, the infection consultant. She once treated patients in South Africa with similar viruses and covered up with body gear to protect herself.

"I'm not sure the CDC can do anything differently—because what is the public going to do, knowing that it's contagious? What are we going to do?" Segal asked.

Others question the CDC's communication strategy.

MacGregor-Skinner said the use of text messaging to trace contacts with infected individuals was key to containing the virus in Port Harcourt, Nigeria, where he recently was based.

"Contact tracing is the key," he said. "Let's not stigmatize people who have been in contact with this patient."

Researching, Preparing

Federal authorities at the National Institutes of Health have yet to begin human testing of an investigational vaccine to treat Ebola.

"We need to be sure the vaccines are safe and effective before they're used widely," said Dr. Beth Bell, director of the National Center for Emerging and Zoonotic Infectious Diseases.

Experts say it's only a matter of time before Ebola hits cities such as Pittsburgh. When that happens, it is important for hospitals to be prepared with equipment and infection control training for health care workers.

"Every city in the world, technically, could have an Ebola case and should be preparing at the hospital level," said Dr. Amesh Adalja, an infectious disease physician at UPMC. "I don't think this outbreak is going to be over for quite some time."

Adalja said Ebola is on everyone's mind because it has been portrayed in movies that strike fear and provoke people's imaginations.

"Ebola has this mystique about it. It's a mysterious disease that comes out of nowhere. It's very deadly, very scary, and then it disappears," Adalja said.

Confronting the Global Threat Posed by Ebola by Investing in Global Public Goods

David Gartner

David Gartner is a nonresident fellow with the Development Assistance and Governance Initiative at the Brookings Institution.

The first Ebola death in the United States makes clear that global health challenges in the 21st century can no longer be considered local problems. While the United States government just moved to require airport screening for fevers for passengers travelling from West Africa, this is unlikely to be an effective strategy. Given the extended incubation period of the virus, even travelers who might have Ebola are likely to be asymptomatic. As the Director of the Centers for Disease Control and Prevention (CDC) Thomas Frieden explained, "The plain truth is we can't make the risk zero until the outbreak is controlled in West Africa." The only effective strategy for the United States and other countries to defend against Ebola is to invest in the global public goods needed to defeat Ebola in Liberia, Sierra Leone, and Guinea.

Public Health Failure

The Ebola catastrophe did not have to happen but instead was a result of multiple failures when it comes to disease surveillance, vaccine innovation, and the emergency public health response. It reveals that we need different strategies to prevent the next outbreak and to deal with the exponential growth of the current pandemic. As I have found in my research, effective global health responses require distinct approaches to solving collective action failures—the same type of failures that are at the root of the current crisis. Without these failures, the world would already have an Ebola vaccine, the initial outbreak would not have festered for three months without anyone figuring out what was happening, and a serious global response would not have been delayed by as much as nine months as the epidemic spun out of control.

The first failure that gave rise to the current Ebola crisis is the failure of adequate disease surveillance. It looks like the first victim of this outbreak was a 2-year-old boy in a remote Guinean village. His mysterious death in December 2013 was followed by similar deaths within that region and across the country before experts from Doctors Without Borders identified the culprit as Ebola. If Guinea's extremely weak health system had a more robust system of surveillance this disease could have been stopped in its tracks before it ever reached Liberia or Sierra Leone. This weakest-link challenge resulting from limited disease surveillance capacity within Guinea reveals that without strengthening health systems in many of the poorest countries in the world, global health responses will continue to be behind the curve.

> *Despite the many failures which contributed to the current catastrophe, there are some important signs that Ebola can be defeated.*

Even after Ebola was identified, another six months passed before any country with the resources to adequately respond to the pandemic stepped up to the plate in a major way. In September [2014], President [Barack] Obama committed the United States to building Ebola treatment units and training health care workers. Despite this important effort, the global response still faces a shortfall of over $300 million even as the cost of the epidemic continues to grow dramatically. Only three countries have committed more than $20 million and most countries have contributed nothing at all. This problem of aggregate effort is central to the challenge of financing a sufficient emergency public health response in the affected countries to contain the virus.

Vaccine Needed

Perhaps the most dramatic failure is the fact that nearly 40 years after the discovery of the Ebola virus there is still no effective vaccine. Leading scientists suggest that the technical challenges to creating a vaccine are relatively modest and two potentially promising vaccine candidates already exist. Yet the lack of a sufficient financial incentive for drug manufacturers meant that neither vaccine candidate was pushed forward to human trials until very recently. In the face of this dramatic market failure, a "single-best effort" investment by the United States in vaccine innovation can make a dramatic difference for the entire world.

Despite the many failures which contributed to the current catastrophe, there are some important signs that Ebola can be defeated. The spread of Ebola to Nigeria was quickly contained in Africa's most populous country thanks to a rapid response that included strict quarantines for suspected cases, the temporary closing of schools, and screening for thousands of others. The survival of courageous health workers from the United States and elsewhere suggests there may be promise in new treatments that the United States is now investing in bringing to human trials. The possibility of blood transfusions from those who have survived may be the most effective treatment at present. The development of a rapid diagnostic to detect Ebola, which is within reach, could dramatically simplify the process of identifying those suffering from the virus and implementing appropriate public health responses.

The reality remains, however, that none of this will be possible without a dramatically ramped up global response. Liberia alone needs hundreds of additional foreign medical staff just to treat those now infected. More than 8,000 people have been infected so far and without extraordinary efforts, the CDC estimates that this number could grow to as many as 1.4 million by January [2015]. Thousands of others are now dying from untreated malaria or other illnesses as a consequence of a pandemic that is devastating the economies of the region and causing significant food insecurity. In the short term, a global aggregate effort to finance an emergency response and provide trained health care workers is essential to prevent Ebola from reaching many more countries. In the long-term, only by strengthening the health care systems and disease surveillance capacity in West Africa and other low-income regions and by investing in innovation to catalyze effective vaccines for potentially devastating viruses such as Ebola can the United States and the rest of the world be protected.

Why We Won't Have an Ebola Cure or Vaccine for Years

Jeffrey Young

Jeffrey Young is a health-care reporter at Huffington Post.

The world has known about Ebola for almost 40 years, yet there's no cure or vaccine on the market.

That could change amid worldwide attention to the ongoing outbreak of the virus in West Africa, which has claimed more than 3,000 lives already, and the first diagnosis of a patient with the disease in the United States. But not for a few more years—at least.

Ebola a Low Priority

Why have the scientific community, the pharmaceutical industry and world governments failed so far to come up with a way to treat or prevent this ghastly illness? Because the scientific and economics challenges are stark, and the experimental medicines available, even those already being used to treat Ebola patients, haven't been proved to be effective or safe.

Drug and vaccine development is characterized by failure, a fact that's easy to forget when so many miracle cures exist.

And despite gruesome symptoms including bleeding from the eyes, ears and mouth, and the fact that most Ebola patients die, 33 outbreaks of the virus had killed just over 1,500 people since 1976 before the current crisis, according to the Centers for Disease Control and Prevention.

This not only means that other diseases with broader reaches, such as HIV and AIDS, take precedence in scientific research, but that drug companies have had virtually no financial incentive to spend millions of dollars on medicines and inoculations for so few people—especially people who lack the means to pay for it.

"There's nothing magical about getting a drug or a vaccine for Ebola. We likely would've had it years ago if there were major investments on the part of a company," said Anthony Fauci, director of the National Institute of Allergy and Infectious Diseases at the National Institutes of Health in Bethesda, Maryland. "The scientific challenges are not profound."

The scale and horrors of Ebola in West Africa, combined with diagnoses in Western countries such as the U.S., will spur greater interest among drug developers and speed possible treatments to market, Fauci predicted.

"What you'll see now is that this dramatic, highly publicized outbreak of Ebola is going to catalyze a lot of interest in the field of making antivirals for these types of diseases," Fauci said.

Experts cautioned against expecting the kind of quick turnaround of a cure or vaccine [for Ebola] performed by scientists in the movies.

A handful of pharmaceutical and biotechnology companies already were working on medicines, vaccinations and tests for Ebola, many of which received funding from the National Institutes of Health.

ZMapp, under development by a California firm called Mapp Biopharmaceutical, has garnered attention since the African outbreak began and the company depleted its stock by shipping medicine overseas. The U.S. government, the Bill & Melinda Gates Foundation and the Wellcome Trust are working with the company and another firm to boost production of the experimental treatment, *The New York Times* reported.

In addition, a Massachusetts company, Sarepta Therapeutics, is working on another drug, as are Canada's Tekmira Pharmaceuticals and North Carolina's BioCryst Pharmaceuticals. A unit of British pharmaceutical giant GlaxoSmithKline is researching a vaccine, and Japan's Fujifilm is eyeing an existing flu medicine as an Ebola treatment.

In spite of these efforts and the intensified push from Western governments—not to mention newly vigorous interest from investors—experts cautioned against expecting the kind of quick turnaround of a cure or vaccine performed by scientists in the movies.

"We are certainly not at the beginning of these developments, but we're probably still realistically somewhere between five and 10 years away from having something that's on the market," said Ted Ross, program director for vaccines and viral immunity at the Vaccine and Gene Therapy Institute of Florida in Port Saint Lucie.

Three or Four Years

The timeline could be shortened to three or four years with a concerted push by governments, amplified by the efforts of wealthy charities and other nongovernmental organizations, Ross said.

Governments have a lot of weight, and money, to throw around, which has enabled scientists and pharmaceutical companies to make relatively rapid strides when the focus is there.

Fauci cited two significant examples as precedent. The massive global push to study HIV and AIDS led not only to treatments for that ailment, but to progress in developing drugs for other diseases, such as Hepatitis C, he said. More recently, concern about new, unpreventable strains of influenza spurred advances in flu research that may lead to the creation of a single shot that can protect against all forms of the virus, he said.

That doesn't mean it's easy, even with all possible support from governments, pharmaceutical companies or anyone else. Inventing medicines and vaccines and diagnostic tests is difficult, takes time and is more likely to fail than succeed, Ross said.

"It really takes almost a decade from concept to finally put the drug into a vial that you're ready to hand to a physician or a nurse," Ross said. "Very few drugs ever make it to market."

Even if you have a drug that is effective, it really sometimes comes down to the economics of it.

Scientists must follow a basic set of procedures throughout that can take an unknown amount of time and pose challenges all along, any one of which could scuttle the entire enterprise, Ross said.

It starts out with the basic, fundamental research of understanding what the disease is, how it works and how it might be counteracted. If those stages are successful and researchers have an idea of a way to attack the disease, they have to test it on animals to see whether it works at all, and whether it's safe. Before a treatment or vaccine can be tested on living humans, scientists must conduct two rounds of research on human cells and tissue, first for safety and then for effectiveness. If all of that is successful, a drug company then has to get approval from the Food and Drug Administration and regulators in other countries to sell the product, which can take years.

During those painstaking steps, researchers and drugmakers always have to think about money. "It costs millions of dollars to do human trials," Ross said.

"Even if you have a drug that is effective, it really sometimes comes down to the economics of it. If it's going to cost you way more than what a person can afford, they're not going to be able to manufacture it," Ross said. "There won't be a market for it."

Treating Ebola as a Military Issue Is Endangering Safety and Health

Yanzhong Huang

Yanzhong Huang is senior fellow for global health at the Council on Foreign Relations.

The Ebola outbreak in West Africa, the largest of its kind in history, has been responsible for more than 15,000 cases, including more than 5,400 reported deaths as of late November [2014]. Unlike the responses to previous Ebola outbreaks, political and public health leaders have upped the ante by explicitly framing the disease in national and international security terms. Margaret Chan, the director general of the World Health Organization (WHO), spoke of "a threat to national security well beyond the outbreak zones," and U.S. President Barack Obama described the outbreak as "a growing threat to regional and global security."

Securitizing the Virus

Although public health experts dismiss the prospect of a worldwide pandemic or even a sustained outbreak in the United States, Americans were told that the United States' national security would be threatened by both an Ebola-triggered state collapse in Africa and a large number of panicked people (some of whom also carry the virus) flooding into the United States from Central and South America.

By calling for tighter border security in combating Ebola, politicians and military officials placed the virus on par with hard security threats such as ISIS terrorists [in Iraq and Syria].

Yanzhong Huang, "The Downside of Securitizing the Ebola Virus," Council on Foreign Relations, November 25, 2014. Copyright © 2014 by the Council on Foreign Relations. Reprinted with permission.

In a move not seen in the 2009 H1N1 [virus] pandemic, which killed an estimated 284,000 people, Obama announced the establishment of a new military command in Liberia and committed nearly 4,000 troops to the afflicted region.

The United States is not the only country that has "securitized" the Ebola outbreak, a political process that has presented the virus as an existential threat requiring actions outside the normal bounds of political procedure. In Sierra Leone, the defense minister, not the health minister, was put in charge of the "fight" against Ebola. In Liberia, President Ellen Johnson Sirleaf imposed a state of emergency that closed schools and markets and restricted people's movements.

> *The United States, Canada, Russia, and China have all claimed to have developed or accelerated clinical trials of vaccines and/or treatments for the [Ebola] virus.*

This is not the first time an infectious disease has been framed as a national security challenge. Beginning in the 1990s, U.S. Vice President Al Gore cited HIV/AIDS as a security problem that "threatens not just individual citizens but the very institutions that define and defend the character of a society." Similarly in 2005–2006, some U.S. lawmakers juxtaposed avian influenza H5N1 with nuclear proliferation, rogue states, and global terrorism and viewed it as a direct threat to security and prosperity in the United States. By mobilizing security apparatuses to deal with a virus that is not easily transmissible, the securitization of infectious diseases has been pushed to a new level.

Fear, Anxiety, Overreaction

Defining Ebola as a security threat has raised political awareness about an otherwise neglected health problem and galvanized strong national and international responses to the outbreak. Fear of a common threat (what political scientist Arthur

Stein termed the "dilemma of common aversions") creates a situation in which countries must act together to avoid mutually undesirable outcomes. In mid-November, approximately $1.2 billion had been committed to the fight against Ebola in the three most-hit countries. U.S. Ambassador to the United Nations Samantha Power said international aid efforts and awareness campaigns helped slow the spread of the virus in West Africa.

On the domestic front, the securitization of Ebola has also triggered dynamics that have persuaded policymakers worldwide to formulate a range of preparedness plans and policy actions aimed at strengthening disease surveillance and response capacities and speeding up work on an anti-Ebola vaccines and medicines. The United States, Canada, Russia, and China have all claimed to have developed or accelerated clinical trials of vaccines and/or treatments for the virus. Furthermore, since countries hardest hit by the virus have poor state capacity, sending the military (which has comparatively strong organizational and command-and-control capabilities) is instrumental not only to help build much needed treatment centers and mobile labs, but also to coordinate multisectoral and multinational efforts to contain the virus.

The same mode of discourse on Ebola and security nevertheless may increase public fear of the disease to a level disproportionate to actual disease-caused morbidity and mortality. As of November 14, 99.8 percent of the cases had been found in three Western African countries (Guinea, Liberia, and Sierra Leone), and Spain and the United States were the only two non-African countries reporting Ebola cases. And in the United States, only four confirmed cases thus far have been found, and none of those who contracted the virus in the country have died. Yet fear and anxiety spread much faster than the virus in the United States. The problem is that in evaluating risks posed by an infectious disease, public health professionals have to consider the compound probability of contracting the disease and succumbing to its effects, but the general public tends to respond only to the likelihood of death in the event the disease is contracted. In a securitized policy context, with the threat of an infectious disease heightened by political leaders and media outlets, this perception gap has been further expanded, leading to panic and overreaction to the disease.

Securitization tends to push disease responses away from civil society toward military organizations and law enforcement agencies that have the power to override freedoms and civil liberties.

If the securitization efforts are joined by more drastic government interventions, the fear and overreaction could impact the national and global economy. According to the World Bank, the vast majority of economic losses during a disease outbreak are attributed to uncoordinated and irrational efforts by the public to avoid infection.

Mismanaging the Risks

The logic of securitization often works against effective risk management. A study published in the medical journal *The Lancet* estimated that the risk of Ebola spreading to the United States was only 13 percent of the risk of spread to the United Kingdom or France combined. The securitization approach, however, often leads to heavy-handed government interventions that do not differentiate actual risks posed to communities, states, and populations.

Indeed, it was not until the end of October that the U.S. Centers for Disease Control (CDC) adopted targeted strategies that classify individuals into different risk categories. Also in October, Canada announced it would deny entry to foreign nationals traveling from Ebola hot spots in West Africa. Similarly, the governors of New York, New Jersey, and Illinois announced plans to quarantine all medical personnel returning from Ebola-ridden countries in West Africa. The same logic may fuel discrimination against certain groups of people. Some policymakers have called for tighter border restrictions, for fear that immigrants from Latin America may be carrying the disease, even though no confirmed cases have been reported in the region.

It would be more responsible and constructive to adopt a risk-based approach that tailors government interventions to the actual risks posed by the disease.

Second, by pinpointing an existential threat that requires an emergency response, securitization tends to push disease responses away from civil society toward military organizations and law enforcement agencies that have the power to override freedoms and civil liberties. This is especially troublesome if the military is used to enforce quarantine or other containment measures and target sick and exposed people—not the virus itself—as the presumed enemy. But even if the military is not involved in rounding up individuals suspected of carrying the virus, a securitized policy context could have the unintended effect of breaking the trust between the general public and public health authorities by encouraging civilians to shun public health officials and health workers. This has been a major concern in West Africa, where lack of trust in the government is a major factor behind the surge of the Ebola cases and deaths. In countries hardest hit by Ebola, health workers and clinics have come under attack from panicked residents who mistakenly blamed health workers for bringing in the virus.

Finally, securitization of the outbreak is not necessarily conducive for long-term health system capacity building in West Africa. It implies that health is less important than security and can only be justified in term of its impact on security.

Once the epidemic tapers off, and the media spotlight is gone, the perceived impact of the virus on security would no longer be sufficient to justify strong political commitments and extraordinary public health measures. Fatigue and complacency could combine to cause problems for sustaining existing anti-Ebola programs.

Balancing Public Health Challenges

Moreover, since "securitization" tends to focus on a particular disease, it also raises questions of fungibility and scalability. When huge resources are diverted to Ebola prevention and control, other public health challenges such as malaria and tuberculosis are neglected. The investment in vertical, disease-specific programs may not be able to translate into gains in overall health system strengthening. This we have seen in the aftermath of China's 2002–2003 SARS [Severe Acute Respiratory Syndrome] crisis: the 1,200-bed hospital built to treat SARS patients was quietly abandoned once the crisis was over.

To sum up, while securitization might be necessary to address the ongoing Ebola outbreak, it may have negative impacts on socioeconomic stability, civil-military relations, risk management, and long-term health system capacity building. Instead of promoting a securitization approach to handling acute disease outbreaks, a more effective approach would be to frame disease control as a global public good. Under this new approach, countries would be obliged to contribute to an international capacity building fund—administered by the World Health Organization—and to use that fund to strengthen disease surveillance and response capacities in countries that fail to meet the requirements of the revised International Health Regulations. With a more robust health system capacity, these countries will be able to nip a rising pathogen in the bud. And if an outbreak was to evolve into a Public Health Emergency of International Concern as Ebola has, it should trigger an institutionalized (not securitized) arrangement that could lead to a surge of international assistance.

On the domestic front, it would be more responsible and constructive to adopt a risk-based approach that tailors government interventions to the actual risks posed by the disease. The implementation of this approach, when combined with effective international collaboration, would maximize the protection of domestic population health while minimizing the disturbance the virus-spawned fear may cause to the economy and the society.

Five Public Health Threats in Texas Scarier than Ebola

Anna C. Dragsbaek

Anna C. Dragsbaek is president and chief executive officer of the Immunization Partnership.

There's no doubt about it: Ebola is scary.

The disease has a high mortality rate and no known cure. No vaccine is available to halt its spread. And now it has arrived in Dallas—the first confirmed case in the U.S.

A media firestorm is brewing, and the public is understandably concerned. But the threat of Ebola spreading in the U.S. is nominal. Highly advanced disease surveillance systems, well-developed quarantine and isolation laws, adequate hygiene and sanitation, and top-notch medical services will keep the U.S. from facing a crisis similar to the one sweeping through West Africa.

But that doesn't mean we shouldn't be worried about infectious diseases. In fact, there are at least five other preventable threats right now that are far more menacing—and Texans would be wise to pay close attention to them.

1. Influenza: Last year, widespread influenza in Texas led to the deaths of 20 children, most of whom were unvaccinated. The flu vaccine is widely available through clinics, workplaces, churches, commercial pharmacies and schools, but influenza vaccination rates among adults in Texas remain low. In Texas, only one in three young adults (who are most likely to have small children in the home and to transmit the virus to them) were immunized against influenza last season.

Children died not from a rare infectious disease but from a vaccine-preventable disease that we didn't protect them from.

2. Pertussis: In 2013. Texas reported 3,985 cases of pertussis, or whooping cough—more than any other state in the U.S. This disease is particularly dangerous for infants, which is why the vaccine is recommended for pregnant women and caregivers. Yet only about one in four adults who live with infants have been immunized against it.

In 2011–12, nearly 30,000 children in Texas schools were unvaccinated, most of them for non-medical reasons likely due to fears about vaccine safety.

---

3. Neglected tropical diseases: Chagas, Chikungunya, dengue and other so-called neglected tropical diseases, or NTDs, are all circulating in Texas. Several of these diseases cause long-term disabilities and even heart defects. Yet despite the potentially devastating impact of NTDs, doctors don't always diagnose them properly, and many cases go unreported due to inadequate surveillance and a lack of funding for vaccine development. To determine the true burden of disease, the Texas Legislature should appropriate funds to expand the capacities of existing clinics to detect a host of NTD threats.

4. Measles: So far this year, 595 cases of measles have been reported nationally—as many as the previous five years combined and the highest number in 20 years. Texas has seen its share of cases, with outbreaks in Tarrant County and a few cases in Houston. Unlike Ebola, measles is an airborne disease and is highly contagious. Simply being in the same room with someone who has measles can—and almost always does—cause an unvaccinated person to be infected. A highly effective vaccine nearly eradicated the disease, but it has recently made a comeback due to the surge in children who are not fully immunized, which leads me to the fifth threat:

5. Vaccine refusal: Texas allows parents to opt out of vaccines for their children based on personal beliefs. This means that your child could be in a school with unvaccinated children, who would present a significant risk of spreading diseases like measles, chicken pox, meningitis or some other vaccine-preventable disease if there were an outbreak. In 2011–12, nearly 30,000 children in Texas schools were unvaccinated, most of them for non-medical reasons likely due to fears about vaccine safety that have been thoroughly refuted by the medical community. But due to regulations about how data are collected and stored, Texas parents don't have access to any information about the immunization rates in their children's schools. The parents of a child with an immune-suppressing illness have rights, too. The virus of vaccine refusal is based on pseudoscience, but it's spreading every day in Texas, and we're poised for a preventable tragedy.

Having spent six years living and working in Sierra Leone in a rural missionary hospital and later as a relief worker during the civil war, I've been watching the spread of Ebola in my former home with a heavy heart and a deep understanding of the overwhelming challenges facing the country. Given Sierra Leone's brutally hot climate and lack of resources and public health infrastructure, it's no surprise that the epidemic has quickly escalated to a public health emergency and humanitarian crisis.

But we can and will avert widespread outbreak in the U.S. The real threat is complacency and a disregard for the scientific evidence of vaccine safety. Texas must increase funding to fight vaccine-preventable disease, reform our laws to prioritize public health and respond to constant threats that jeopardize the health of our community.

Vaccines and Treatments Are Being Developed to Treat Ebola

World Health Organization

The World Health Organization is the international public health arm of the United Nations.

This Q&A provides answers to questions about clinical trials and evaluations of potential vaccines, therapies, and diagnostics for Ebola virus disease.

Vaccines

Is there a vaccine to protect against Ebola virus disease [EVD]?

At this time, there are no vaccines to protect against EVD licensed for use in humans. Clinical trials for several candidate vaccines are in various phases and a safe and effective vaccine is hoped for by the end of 2015.

Which vaccines are in development?

Currently, two vaccine candidates are entering efficacy trials in humans: ChAd3-ZEBOV, developed by GlaxoSmithKline (GSK), in collaboration with the US National Institute of Allergy and Infectious Diseases (NIAID) and rVSV-ZEBOV, developed by NewLink Genetics and Merck Vaccines USA, in collaboration with the Public Health Agency of Canada. Both have been shown to be safe and well tolerated in humans in Phase I clinical trials.

Johnson & Johnson, in association with Bavarian Nordic, is developing a 2-dose vaccination approach for Ebola using different vaccines for the first and second doses. This approach is known as heterologous prime-boost. The two vaccine candidates are known as Ad26-EBOV and MVA-EBOV.

Novavax, a biotech company in the US, is developing a recombinant protein Ebola vaccine candidate based on the Guinea 2014 Ebola virus strain and is currently beginning Phase I human clinical trials in Australia.

The Russian Federal Ministry of Health is developing a recombinant influenza candidate Ebola vaccine, as well as other approaches. The recombinant influenza candidate is scheduled to start Phase I trials in the second half of 2015. Other products in development include an oral adenovirus platform (Vaxart), an alternative vesicular stomatitis virus candidate (Profectus Biosciences), an alternative recombinant protein (Protein Sciences), a DNA vaccine (Inovia) and a recombinant rabies vaccine (Jefferson University).

There is also an Ebola vaccine candidate going through clinical testing in China; WHO [World Health Organization] is actively seeking further information on this candidate vaccine.

What were the outcomes from the Phase I vaccine clinical trials?

Of the pre-existing medicines that were considered for repurposing to treat Ebola, several are either being tested or considered for testing in patients with EVD or have already been used in patients with EVD.

Both vaccines were deemed safe and were well tolerated in the volunteers who participated in Phase I clinical trials. There were no serious adverse events. A few volunteers in the rVSV-ZEBOV trials in Geneva, Switzerland, reported temporary arthritis with no evidence of auto-immunity. This resulted in a halt to the Geneva trial so that safety monitoring and oversight could be strengthened. The trial restarted in January 2015.

Which other treatments, therapies, or devices are available or being evaluated?

Assessments of national capacities for ensuring the safety of blood products outside of clinical trial settings and plans for recovery and strengthening of national blood transfusion services in the affected countries are being developed.

Drugs and Medicines

Of the pre-existing medicines that were considered for repurposing to treat Ebola, several are either being tested or considered for testing in patients with EVD or have already been used in patients with EVD. A few other therapies have also been considered for use in treatment, but have been deemed not to be appropriate for further investigation. Of the novel products, like FX06 and Zmab, some have shown initial promise in models and a few have been administered to a small number of Ebola patients on a compassionate basis. However, these cases are too few to permit any conclusion regarding safety and efficacy. Several drugs have also been used in clinical settings without prior review by WHO, including amiodarone, atorvastatin + irbesartan +/− clomiphene.

The drugs have been evaluated by the WHO Science and Technical Advisory Committee on Emergency Ebola Interventions (STAC-EE) and categorized as follows:

- Drugs already under evaluation in formal clinical trials in West Africa.

- Drugs that have been prioritized for testing in human efficacy trials, but for which such trials are not yet underway.

- Drugs that have already been given to patients for compassionate reasons or in ad hoc trials.

- Drugs that demonstrate promising anti-Ebola activity in-vitro or in mouse models, but for which additional data should be generated prior to proceeding to clinical trials.

- Drugs that had been prioritized or considered for prioritization and have now been deprioritized based on new data or more detailed analysis of old data.

WHO is working with all relevant stakeholders on each of the potential therapies and vaccines to continue to accelerate identification, verification, development, and, if safety and efficacy are found, deployment. . . .

Diagnostics

How is Ebola virus disease (EVD) diagnosed?

Integral to the safe and effective treatment of EVD is the need for appropriate personal protective equipment and essential medicines for providing supportive care to persons with Ebola.

The symptoms for EVD are similar to the onset of many diseases, including influenza and malaria. The best way to diagnose whether someone with suggestive symptoms is infected with EVD is by taking a body sample, such as blood, and sending it to a laboratory that is properly equipped to handle potential Ebola specimens. In some cases, this may be a biosafety level (BSL) 3 or 4 laboratory in a neighbouring city or country. In field situations, mobile laboratories can be established in order to reduce the time between transport of the specimens and return of results. In the case of EVD, the delay caused by the need to transport specimens creates significant logistical problems with the management of potential but unconfirmed cases of EVD. . . .

What other devices or equipment are available for treatment of EVD?

Integral to the safe and effective treatment of EVD is the need for appropriate personal protective equipment and essential medicines for providing supportive care to persons with Ebola.

What are the ethical considerations for use of unregistered interventions?

On 11 August 2014, WHO convened an Ethics Panel to consider and assess the ethical implications of the potential use of unregistered interventions. The panel reached consensus that in the particular circumstances of this outbreak, and provided certain conditions are met, it is ethical to offer unproven interventions for which the safety and efficacy have not yet been demonstrated in humans as potential treatment or prevention. Key conditions relate to the evidence and ethical basis for the assessment of each intervention. There should be a strong scientific basis for the hypothesis that the intervention will be effective against EVD in humans: the unregistered interventions to be offered should have been demonstrated to be safe and efficacious in relevant animal models, and in particular, in non-human primates. In addition, use of such interventions should be based on the best possible assessment of risk and benefit from the information available at a given time.

Ethical criteria must guide the provision of such interventions and should include: transparency about all aspects of care; informed consent; freedom of choice; confidentiality; respect for the person; preservation of dignity; and involvement of the community. The panel advised that there is a moral obligation to collect and share all data generated, including from treatments provided for compassionate use. In addition, several areas were identified that need more analysis and discussion:

- ethical ways to gather data while striving to provide optimal care under the prevailing circumstances;

- ethical criteria to prioritize the use of unregistered experimental therapies and vaccines; and

- ethical criteria for achieving fair distribution of therapies and vaccines in communities and among countries.

CHAPTER 2

Should Vaccines Against Deadly Viruses Be Compulsory?

Chapter Preface

In the United States, there is a small but vocal group of anti-vaccination parents, or "anti-vaxxers," who refuse to immunize their children against dangerous diseases like measles and mumps. There are also anti-vaxxers in Australia; the government there estimates that about thirty-nine thousand children under seven are not vaccinated because of parental objections. But while the United States has a patchwork of vaccine regulations by state, Australia has begun to move forward on national efforts to increase vaccine rates and punish parents who refuse to vaccinate their children.

The most important recent pro-vaccination initiative involves welfare benefits. Australian prime minister Tony Abbott has declared that in 2015, parents who refuse to vaccinate their children will no longer be eligible for welfare benefits. This could cost many families around $9,000 US dollars per year. There will be some religious exemptions, but restrictions on other conscientious or ethical objections will be tightened.

Some parents are concerned that vaccines may have dangerous side-effects. But Abbott, in a joint statement with social services minister Scott Morrison, said that the choice not to vaccinate "is not supported by public policy or medical research nor should such actions be supported by taxpayers in the form of child care payments."[1]

Jenna Price, a columnist for *The Canberra Times*, generally supports the policy but is concerned that it might end up targeting the wrong people. Some people who do not vaccinate are committed anti-vaxxers, she says, but others are "the dis-

1. Quoted in BBC News, "Australia to Stop Welfare Cash of Anti-Vaccine Parents," April 12, 2015. http://www.bbc.com/news/world-australia-32274107.

enfranchised, the disadvantaged, the disorganised."[2] This group may fail to get vaccines because they have trouble getting to doctors, or simply because they aren't educated about the virtues or necessity of vaccines. Price argues that cutting off benefits is not a good way to push such people to get vaccines. Instead, she suggests more funding for community outreach programs. She argues that money saved in welfare payouts should be funneled to such programs.

Whatever the mix of policy solutions, the push for more vaccination seems to reflect a weakening of the anti-vaccination movement in Australia in recent years. The Australian Vaccination-Skeptics Network (AVN), the largest anti-vaccination organization in Australia, has seen a significant drop in funding and membership since 2011.[3] Media organizations have been less willing to turn to it for expertise as well, and in 2014 the New South Wales state government deprived the AVN of its charitable status. Along with the new welfare policies, Australia hopes that the waning of AVN's influence will help to increase vaccination rates throughout the country.

The rest of this chapter looks at current controversies about whether or not vaccines for viruses like measles should be compulsory.

2. Jenna Price, "Anti-Vaccine Battle Plan All Wrong," WAtoday.com.au, April 14, 2015. http://www.watoday.com.au/comment/antivaccine-battle-plan-all-wrong-20150414 -1mjqvp.html.

3. Michael Safi, "Australia's Anti-Vaccine Movement in Decline as Membership Drops Off," *Guardian*, January 6, 2015. http://www.theguardian.com/society/2015/jan/06 /australias-anti-vaccine-movement-decline-membership-drops-off.

Measles Can Kill, and It's Spreading. Sue Parents Who Didn't Vaccinate? Absolutely

Dan Diamond

Dan Diamond is a contributor to Forbes *and the executive editor of the Advisory Board's* Daily Briefing, *a popular health-care newsletter.*

I heard it over dinner at a friend's house. I talked about it on a call with a scientist. I discussed it while waiting for public health officials to issue an update on the measles outbreak.

The same murmured question, the same growing fear.

What happens if a child dies because some parents decided not to vaccinate their own kid?

What happens if it's *my* child?

The Parents Causing the Measles Outbreak

Thankfully, it's still a hypothetical. But there's reason to worry: More than 100 people in six states are now sick with the measles, in an outbreak that can be traced directly back to Disneyland. Dozens of newborns have been put into isolation.

Public health officials from California to Chicago are warning that this outbreak is only going to grow.

And there's also reason to be angry: This outbreak began with Americans who chose to skip getting vaccinated. But now, they're not the only ones getting sick.

Americans forgot to be worried, because the vaccination rate in the United States was so high for decades. But measles isn't a harmless childhood disease.

First, it's fast-spreading. Measles has a reproduction rate of 12 to 18 people for every person it infects, a high R-number that's helped it spread despite our nation's 90%-plus vaccination rate. (Compare the measles outbreak to the Ebola scare, where thousands of Americans were exposed but just two Americans ultimately infected in the United States: A pair of nurses who had cared for an Ebola patient, in close proximity and with inadequate protection.)

Most importantly, measles carries real risks: brain damage for some, death for others.

In parts of California, the vaccine exemption rate for young children is at least 13%—higher than in Ghana, where it's 11%.

About 1-in-5,000 people who aren't protected from measles will die from it. More than 300 people die from measles around the world every day, mostly children.

To put that another way: If you're unvaccinated, you're about 35,000 times more likely to die from measles than you are to win at PowerBall.

And the rate of unvaccinated people has been steadily rising in the United States. In parts of California, the vaccine exemption rate for young children is at least 13%—higher than in Ghana, where it's 11%.

Why Are Vaccine Rates Low?

There's been much debate, and even irritation, over why so many people are unvaccinated in the United States. After all, access to vaccines is widespread, and federally subsidized. Blame a mix of these five key culprits:

1. Some parents are deliberately opting out. These anti-vaxxers, to use the slang term, cut across the social spectrum. But they're linked by a desire to avoid vaccinating their kids, and it's not for medical necessity. Some are wealthy and choose "natural" lifestyles that reject modern drugs and vaccines. Some have religious objections. Others fear that vaccines cause medical complications like autism—sometimes helped by physicians who unforgivably feed their paranoia. But to be clear: there is no link between the measles vaccine and autism. None. Zero.

These parents can obtain vaccination exemptions, and the restrictions vary by state. Importantly, some state legislatures are trying to make it easier for these parents to get an exemption, although as [British writer] Tim Worstall points out, lawmakers have largely failed to do so.

2. Others didn't get vaccinated because it wasn't an option. Some people end up unvaccinated by accident—they lack access to health care, misunderstand the importance of the vaccine, or simply didn't have time to go. As social scientist Julie Leask tells Keith Kloor at *Discover* magazine, "it's not just the haves, but the have-nots who don't fully vaccinate."

The more Americans that get vaccinated, the less likely it is that there will be an outbreak here.

---

3. Newborn children are too young to be vaccinated. Here's where it starts getting very, very scary for U.S. parents, as Vox's Sarah Kliff pointed out. In the current outbreak, there are at least six newborns who contracted measles; many more babies are now being placed in isolation. "I'm terribly upset that someone has made a choice that not only affects their child but other people's children," said Jennifer Simon, the mother of a newborn girl that was exposed when a measles patient visited her hospital, and is now stuck in isolation.

4. Many children and adults have other medical issues. Some people *do* have proven medical reactions to vaccines, or compromised immune systems that leave them unprotected. For instance, a 34-year-old man in my circle of friends recently underwent a stem cell transplant—which meant afterwards "he had no immune system and no vaccine history, and had to get his shots on the same schedule as an infant," his wife told me. (At times, the couple had to live apart to avoid their son infecting his father with the chicken pox.)

5. Some people got vaccinated—but for whatever reason, it didn't take. This is the scariest possibility for many U.S. adults: They got the measles vaccine years ago, but because it isn't 100% effective, they're in for a nasty surprise as the outbreak spreads across the nation. For instance, at least five people infected in the Disneyland measles outbreak had received the recommended two-shot vaccination against the measles. One study of recent measles outbreaks suggested that as many as 10% of measles cases occurred in previously vaccinated individuals, Tara Haelle writes. To their credit, many Americans *are* trying to be responsible.

And this matters, because if enough people vaccinate against a preventable disease—the target is more than 95% of the population—we keep our "herd immunity." The more Americans that get vaccinated, the less likely it is that there will be an outbreak here, because a disease like measles just can't get a foothold.

That means it's up to the rest of us to protect the newborns, the ill, the people whose vaccinations secretly aren't effective—they're counting on us to take care of them.

"Unless there is a health reason certified by a physician, all parents have a duty to prevent harm to their children and to others by vaccinating," Arthur Caplan told me. Caplan's a prominent bioethicist at NYU [New York University], and an expert on vaccine policy.

"It is neglect to expose your child to vaccine-preventable disease," he added. "It is selfish to expose my kids to disease."

Why Not Vaccinating Your Kids Might Be a Crime

Caplan's thought a lot about these issues. In 2013, he co-authored a notable paper that argued parents who didn't vaccinate their children should be sued or even prosecuted. And the paper's conclusions about reckless behavior are pretty simple, and evident on their face.

Take drunk driving.

People may have their own beliefs around how and when they drink alcohol—but once they run the risk of harming others, it really is in the state's interest to start legislating rules. How different is that from a preventable outbreak?

There have been a number of lawsuits brought over parents' failure to vaccinate, some of which led to settlements.

"If you choose not to vaccinate your child, and your child infects mine and harms or kills them, I believe you ought be held liable for your choice just as we would do for a drunk driver," Caplan argued.

Nicholas Diamond (no relation), a lawyer who's one of Caplan's co-authors, points out an important nuance: There's a difference between being sued by someone over the measles, and police showing up to arrest you.

The paper "tries to make the case for *civil* liability," Nicholas Diamond told me. "It's not an easy case to make," but the authors and their supporters believe it rests on reasonably solid legal ground. And in support of the authors' argument: There have been a number of lawsuits brought over parents' failure to vaccinate, some of which led to settlements.

But is not vaccinating your kids actually a *crime*?

"Legally, it would be very difficult to make out a criminal case, if we're just looking at the bare bones of how the law treats this sort of scenario," Nicholas Diamond acknowledged. But "a prosecutor with a passion and willingness for the issue could pursue it . . . even if nothing really comes of it, to shift the policy dialogue in favor of vaccination."

It's an idea that feels very populist—when in doubt, file a lawsuit—but it's not universally popular in academia yet.

For instance, Mary Holland, an NYU research scholar who's studied vaccines, argued that it's not always possible to prove where an outbreak began. She also contends that Caplan's recommendations ignore the potential dangers, noting that the industry acknowledges that vaccines can cause injury and even death to some.

But Caplan's argument seems backed up by the science. First, CDC [Centers for Disease Control and Prevention] and other public health officials are incredibly skilled at using contact tracing to track down the source of an outbreak. Patient Zero in any community is usually even easier to find when there's an atypical outbreak like measles.

And [University of California] UC-Hastings professor Dorit Reiss Rubenstein points out that contra Holland, the vaccine injury rate is staggeringly low—less than 0.003% of the vaccine administered.

"Children are safer being vaccinated than driven in a car or being home," she writes.

Trying to educate anti-vaccine parents only forces them to retreat further into their shell.

So What to Do?

Although the measles outbreak has mushroomed, many anti-vaxxers are sticking to their tune, the *Los Angeles Times* reports. So how to change their mind? Some argue that we should spend more money promoting vaccinations. Others say we should lobby anti-vaxxers until they understand they're in the wrong.

But the science suggests it's not that simple.

Brendan Nyhan, an excellent political scientist at Dartmouth University, has done pathbreaking research into convincing anti-vaxxers to back off their flawed ideas.

His team's disturbing findings: Trying to educate anti-vaccine parents only forces them to retreat further into their shell. Attempting to correct false beliefs about vaccines "may be especially likely to be counterproductive," Nyhan dryly notes.

For instance, "when [researchers] gave evidence that vaccines aren't linked to autism, that actually made parents who were already skittish about vaccines *less likely* to get their child one in the future," Dr. Aaron Carroll writes at The Incidental Economist, summarizing Nyhan's research. "When they told a dramatic story about an infant in danger because he wasn't immunized, it *increased* parents' beliefs that vaccines had serious side effects."

"Basically, it was all depressing."

So talking to anti-vaxxers might not work. Public shame might not work. What might?

Turn to the law.

"The real goal [of our paper]—and this is so often difficult in public health—is to utilize the law to affect the right public health changes," Nicholas Diamond said.

"Basic tort law or criminal law can both be tools to affect positive public health changes."

Another way to put that: What might encourage some parents to finally get over their fear of vaccines?

Fear of lawsuits.

School Vaccination Exemptions Should Be Restricted

Emily Oshima Lee, Lindsay Rosenthal, and Gabriel Scheffler

Emily Oshima Lee is a policy analyst with the health policy team at the Center for American Progress (CAP). Lindsay Rosenthal is a former research assistant for women's health and rights and health policy at CAP. Gabriel Scheffler is a former Ford Foundation fellow with the health policy team at CAP.

Vaccination is one of the most cost-effective and successful public health interventions. Each year, vaccines save an estimated 6 million to 9 million lives worldwide, including the lives of 3 million children. In the United States, vaccinations have decreased most vaccine-preventable childhood diseases by more than 95 percent. Vaccines have minimized or eliminated outbreaks of certain diseases that were once lethal to large numbers of people, including measles and polio in the United States and smallpox worldwide. But because the bacteria and viruses that cause diseases still exist, the public health gains achieved through vaccines can only be maintained by ensuring that vaccination rates remain high enough to prevent outbreaks.

Herd Immunity

Vaccines are effective not only because they protect individuals who have been vaccinated but also because they confer a broader protection for communities by establishing "herd immunity." When a sufficiently high proportion of a population is vaccinated against communicable diseases, the entire population can obtain protection. As the number of vaccinated people in a given population increases, the likelihood that a susceptible person will come into contact with an infected person decreases; it ultimately becomes difficult for a disease to maintain a chain of infection. Although the vaccination rate required to achieve herd immunity varies by vaccine, it typically ranges from 80 percent to 95 percent of a given population.

Although all states have vaccination mandates for schoolchildren, in recent years they have granted a growing number of nonmedical exemptions.

Herd immunity is critical for protecting the health of many groups of people who are especially vulnerable to communicable diseases: those who cannot be vaccinated, either because they are too young or because an immunological condition makes vaccination too risky; those who choose—or whose parents choose for them—not to get vaccinated for nonmedical reasons such as religious or personal beliefs; and those who have been vaccinated but whose immunological response is insufficient to protect them from potential infection.

Because children are especially vulnerable to certain diseases and because vaccines help the body to develop disease immunity over time, many vaccines are most effective when administered to children at a young age and based on a recommended immunization schedule. A significant number of children in the United States, however, do not receive the fully recommended schedule of vaccinations. These children fall into two broad categories: the unvaccinated, who do not receive any immunizations, and the undervaccinated, who do not receive the fully recommended vaccine schedule. Unvaccinated and undervaccinated children are socioeconomically and demographically distinct populations, and separate factors account for why they are not fully vaccinated; Generally, children tend to be unvaccinated due to their parents' decision to take advantage of vaccine exemptions, whereas many children are undervaccinated because of barriers to access, such as poverty and the cost of vaccines.

Although all states have vaccination mandates for schoolchildren, in recent years they have granted a growing number of nonmedical exemptions. As a result, the risk of infectious disease outbreaks—especially among children—has increased. Clusters of exemptions have cropped up in certain communities, eliminating those communities' herd immunity and leading to outbreaks of vaccine-preventable diseases.

While the issues of nonvaccination and undervaccination must be addressed to protect children and their communities from significant health risks, this brief focuses solely on children who are not immunized due to parents' use of nonmedical vaccine exemptions. We survey the research on state childhood vaccination mandates and exemption categories, focusing on the role that nonmedical exemptions play in reducing immunization coverage in communities throughout the United States. After reviewing the evidence, we suggest possible responses at the state and federal levels.

[The] loss of immunity increases the risk of infection not only for other exemptors—both nonmedical and medical—but also for some individuals who have been vaccinated since no vaccine is 100 percent effective.

Current Vaccination and Exemption Policies

All states currently require children older than age 5 who attend public school or state-licensed day care facilities to receive a series of vaccinations prior to enrollment, though these requirements vary in terms of the number of vaccines required and the school grades covered. While vaccination mandates exist for certain groups of adults, such as military personnel, employees of certain health care facilities, and immigrants who are seeking permanent residence in the United States, the majority of vaccine mandates apply to children.

Although all state school immunization laws grant medical exemptions for children who are susceptible to adverse effects from vaccination, states have different policies regarding nonmedical exemptions. Every state except Mississippi and West Virginia grants some kind of religious exemption, while 17 states allow for "personal belief" or philosophical exemptions. In addition, the administrative procedures for obtaining nonmedical exemptions are much more lenient in some states than in others. Some states require that parents renew their exemption annually, obtain a signature from a local health department official, notarize their exemption form, or write a personal letter explaining their reasons for refusing vaccination. In other states, however, it is much easier to procure an exemption. In Maryland, for example, as of 2006, parents could obtain a religious exemption simply by signing and submitting a prewritten form. According to one study, in 23 states, school officials were not even authorized to deny exemption requests if the requests fulfilled state requirements.

In practice—because much of the responsibility for enforcing exemption laws falls on school officials—there are additional within-state variations in the types of exemptions granted and the processes for approving exemptions. For example, one study found that even in Massachusetts and Missouri, two states that do not allow for personal-belief exemptions, 18.1 percent and 17.0 percent of schools, respectively, permitted personal-belief exemptions anyway. Administrative procedures can also vary within states. Michigan, for example, has no standard statewide process for granting exemptions. Even among states that do have statewide exemption procedures, there is significant variation in how those policies are enforced at the school level.

The Growth of Nonmedical Vaccine Exemptions

In recent years, there has been an increase in state-level rates of nonmedical exemptions from vaccination mandates for schoolchildren. Nationwide, the ratio of nonmedical exemptions to state vaccination mandates still remains relatively low, but between 1991 and 2004, the mean state-level rate increased from 0.98 percent to 1.48 percent. Perhaps more significantly, clusters of exemptions have emerged in individual communities, eliminating those communities' herd immunity and increasing their risk of experiencing an outbreak. In the community of Ashland, Oregon, for example, the vaccination exemption rate for schoolchildren during the 2001–02 school year was 11 percent, compared with a rate of 2.7 percent for the entire state and 3 percent nationwide. These exemption clusters are dangerous because if enough individuals within a particular community receive exemptions, then the community will lose its herd immunity. In turn, this loss of immunity increases the risk of infection not only for other exemptors—both nonmedical and medical—but also for some individuals who have been vaccinated since no vaccine is 100 percent effective.

> *[The] rise in nonmedical exemptions has contributed to recent outbreaks and increased rates of vaccine-preventable diseases, such as measles, pertussis, and whooping cough.*

There are a number of factors that have influenced the rise in nonmedical exemptions. To some degree, vaccines are victims of their own success; they have reduced the incidence of vaccine-preventable diseases so much that a growing number of people are less concerned about contracting them. At the same time, public concern about the real or perceived adverse health effects from vaccines has increased.

But one important part of the explanation for the rise in nonmedical exemptions lies in the ways that states have constructed exemptions to their vaccination mandates. More specifically, research shows that the states that grant philosophical exemptions or make it easy to apply for exemptions have greater numbers of nonmedical exemptions. In every state for which the Centers for Disease Control and Prevention, or CDC, had data on vaccination rates for children enrolled in kindergarten from 2009 to 2010, the number of philosophical exemptions exceeded the number of religious exemptions. One study estimated that from 2005 to 2011, the rates of nonmedical exemptions in states that allowed philosophical exemptions were 2.5 times higher than in states that only allowed religious exemptions. The rates of exemptions in states with easy exemption policies were 2.3 times higher than in states with rigorous exemption policies. Recent studies, however, suggest that states that only have religious exemptions or moderate or difficult administrative processes may be catching up. In recent years, the growth rate of exemptions in those states outpaced that of states with philosophical exemptions or lenient application procedures.

The Impact of Nonmedical Exemptions on Disease Outbreaks

This rise in nonmedical exemptions has contributed to recent outbreaks and increased rates of vaccine-preventable diseases, such as measles, pertussis, and whooping cough. In 2008, for example, the CDC reported 131 cases of measles in the United States—more than double the yearly average from 2000 to 2007. According to the CDC, "This increase was not the result of a greater number of imported cases, but was the result of greater viral transmission after importation into the United States." The cases occurred "largely among school-aged children who were eligible for vaccination but whose parents chose not to have them vaccinated." A study published in the

Journal of the American Medical Association, or *JAMA*, supports the CDC's conclusion, finding that children who have been exempted from vaccination requirements were 35 times more likely to contract measles than vaccinated children. Another study found that exemptors were more than 22 times as likely to contract measles.

At the same time, pertussis—a disease that was once considered "doomed by science"—has enjoyed a renaissance. The CDC reports that there were more provisional cases reported in 2012 than in any previous year since 1955, and that 49 states and Washington, D.C., reported a rise in reported cases compared to the previous year. In 2010, a pertussis outbreak in California led to the hospitalization of 455 infants and 10 deaths; in 2012, both Washington state and Minnesota reported pertussis epidemics.

States must take primary responsibility for restructuring their vaccine-exemption laws.

Some of this resurgence may be attributable to other factors, such as the acellular pertussis vaccine's diminished long-term effectiveness. But there is a substantial body of research showing that the growth of nonmedical exemptions—itself driven in part by philosophical exemptions and lax exemption procedures—has contributed to an increase in the overall incidence of pertussis and a rise in the risk of pertussis outbreaks in specific communities. Another *JAMA* study, for example, reports that the incidence of pertussis was more than twice as high in states that allow personal-belief exemptions as in states with only religious exemptions, and that states with easy exemption procedures had a incidence of pertussis that was 90 percent higher than states with difficult procedures. Another group of researchers conducted a study of children in Colorado and found that exemptors were nearly six times more likely to contract pertussis.

The impact of nonmedical exemptions has been particularly acute in specific communities where relatively high proportions, or "clusters," of individuals utilized available exemptions. One study found that pockets of high exemption rates exist in Michigan despite its high overall state-level rate of vaccination and that those census tracts with clusters of nonmedical exemptions are three times more likely to have pertussis outbreaks. Another study recently examined rates of religious exemptions in New York state over time and concluded that counties with higher exemption rates had higher rates of reported pertussis compared to low-exemption counties.

Potential State and Federal Responses

The evidence that states with personal-belief exemptions or easy exemption procedures have more nonmedical exemptions and a greater incidence of communicable diseases suggests that modifying these exemption laws would help prevent future outbreaks. States must take primary responsibility for restructuring their vaccine-exemption laws.

One potential reform is for states to eliminate personal-belief exemptions since there is no constitutional requirement for them to grant such exemptions. Eliminating personal-belief exemptions would not affect religious exemptors or individuals with strongly held secular objections. But it could still significantly reduce exemption rates, as there is evidence that many personal-belief exemptions are actually "exemptions of convenience"—meaning that individuals apply for personal-belief exemptions simply because it is easier than fulfilling vaccination requirements.

States could also redesign their exemption-application procedures to ensure that exemptors think more deliberately about their decision. Several states have already started moving in this direction. The Oregon legislature, for example, recently passed a bill requiring that parents demonstrate that they have consulted a physician or watched an online educational video about the risks and benefits of vaccination before sending their unvaccinated children to school. Vermont passed a similar law in 2012, and Washington state passed one in 2011. As with eliminating philosophical exemptions, making exemption procedures more rigorous would not deter those with deeply held convictions against vaccination. But because many exemptions are exemptions of convenience, even minimal administrative requirements have significant impacts on exemption rates.

Vaccines have the capacity to dramatically improve public health, and an individual's refusal to get vaccinated increases the risk of infection for his or her entire community.

To further prevent clusters of vaccine exemptions from forming, state health authorities could do more to monitor and publicize the number of nonmedical exemptions at the county level and focus their education and outreach efforts on counties with exemption clusters. State authorities could also implement uniform statewide processes for granting exemptions and review school exemption policies to ensure that they comply with state law.

The federal government should also support state efforts. The CDC, for example, could publish a model exemption law as a guide for states interested in strengthening their exemption policies. In tandem with state efforts, the CDC could also collect and publicize county-level exemption data, perhaps by publishing a list of those counties with the highest exemption rates and estimating their increased risk of experiencing a disease outbreak. The CDC could help school officials to provide information on school and countywide vaccine-exemption rates to parents so that they are informed about the level of immunization at their children's school. Making this data more transparent and accessible to the public may encourage states or counties with lax vaccine policies to re-examine current laws. It may also foster an understanding among parents that vaccination is important.

Private health insurers could also encourage enrollees to receive cost-free immunizations against preventable diseases by offering premium rebates to individuals who complete their vaccination schedules on time. At a minimum, insurers should send informational materials and reminders to patients about vaccine schedules.

In designing vaccine mandates, governing institutions must balance latitude for individuals to make decisions about their own health and the health of their children with protecting the safety and well-being of the public. Vaccines have the capacity to dramatically improve public health, and an individual's refusal to get vaccinated increases the risk of infection for his or her entire community, including those infants and individuals with medical conditions who do not have the option to receive vaccination. Governments must therefore ensure that individuals who opt out of immunization are informed of the potential consequences of their decision. While more must be done to address other barriers to childhood vaccination, such as the cost and supply of vaccines, the initiatives outlined here are critical steps in addressing a major barrier to effective immunization: excessive parental use of nonmedical exemptions.

Educating Anti-Vaxxers Doesn't Work

Chris Mooney

Chris Mooney is an American journalist and author of The Republican War on Science.

Vaccine denial is dangerous. We know this for many reasons, but just consider one of them: In California in 2010, 10 children died in a whooping cough outbreak that was later linked, in part, to the presence of 39 separate clusters of unvaccinated children in the state. It's that simple: When too many children go unvaccinated, vaccine-preventable diseases spread more easily, and sometimes children die. Nonetheless, as scientifically unfounded fears about childhood vaccines causing autism have proliferated over the past decade or more, a minority of parents are turning to "personal belief exemptions," so-called "alternative vaccine schedules," and other ways to dodge or delay vaccinating their kids.

Talking Sense and Failing

So as a rational person, you might think it would be of the utmost importance to try to *talk some sense into these people*. But there's a problem: According to a major new study in the journal *Pediatrics* trying to do so may actually make the problem worse. The paper tested the effectiveness of four separate pro-vaccine messages, three of which were based very closely on how the Centers for Disease Control and Prevention (CDC) itself talks about vaccines. The results can only be called grim: Not a single one of the messages was successful when it came to increasing parents' professed intent to vaccinate their children. And in several cases the messages actually backfired, either increasing the ill-founded belief that vaccines cause autism or even, in one case, apparently *reducing* parents' intent to vaccinate.

The study, by political scientist Brendan Nyhan of Dartmouth College and three colleagues, adds to a large body of frustrating research on how hard it is to correct false information and get people to accept indisputable facts. Nyhan and one of his coauthors, Jason Reifler of the University of Exeter in the United Kingdom, are actually the coauthors of a much discussed previous study showing that when politically conservative test subjects read a fake newspaper article containing a quotation of George W. Bush asserting that Iraq had weapons of mass destruction, followed by a factual correction stating that this was not actually true, they believed Bush's falsehood more strongly afterwards—an outcome that Nyhan and Reifler dubbed a "backfire effect."

Hearing the frightening narrative actually increased respondents' likelihood of thinking that getting the MMR vaccine will cause serious side effects, from 7.7 percent to 13.8 percent.

Unfortunately, the vaccine issue is prime terrain for such biased and motivated reasoning. Recent research even suggests that a conspiratorial, paranoid mindset prevails among some vaccine rejectionists. To try to figure out how to persuade them, in the new study researchers surveyed a representative sample of 1,759 Americans with at least one child living in their home. A first phase of the study determined their beliefs about vaccines; then, in a follow-up, respondents were asked to consider one of four messages (or a control message) about vaccine effectiveness and the importance of kids getting the MMR (measles, mumps, rubella) vaccine.

The first message, dubbed "Autism correction," was a factual, science-heavy correction of false claims that the MMR vaccine causes autism, assuring parents that the vaccine is "safe and effective" and citing multiple studies that disprove claims of an autism link. The second message, dubbed "Disease risks," simply listed the many risks of contracting the measles, the mumps, or rubella, describing the nasty complications that can come with these diseases. The third message, dubbed "Disease narrative," told a "true story" about a 10-month-old whose temperature shot up to a terrifying 106 degrees after he contracted measles from another child in a pediatrician's waiting room.

All three of these messages are closely based on messages . . . that appear on the CDC website. And then there was a final message that was *not* directly based on CDC communications, dubbed "Disease images." In this case, as a way of emphasizing the importance of vaccines, test subjects were asked to examine three fairly disturbing images of children afflicted with measles, mumps, and rubella. . . .

The results showed that by far, the least successful messages were "Disease narrative" and "Disease images." Hearing the frightening narrative actually *increased* respondents' likelihood of thinking that getting the MMR vaccine will cause serious side effects, from 7.7 percent to 13.8 percent. Similarly, looking at the disturbing images *increased* test subjects' belief that vaccines cause autism. In other words, both of these messages backfired.

Why did that happen? Dartmouth's Nyhan isn't sure, but he comments that "if people read about or see sick children, it may be easier to imagine other kinds of health risks to children, including possibly side effects of vaccines that are actually quite rare." (When it comes to side effects, Nyhan is referring not to autism but to the small minority of cases in which vaccines cause adverse reactions.)

The two more straightforward text-only messages, "Autism correction" and "Disease risks," had more mixed effects. "Disease risks" didn't cause any harm, but it didn't really produce any benefits either.

We should be more careful to test the messages that we use, and to question the intuition that countering misinformation is likely to be the most effective strategy.

As for "Autism correction," it actually worked, among survey respondents as a whole, to somewhat reduce belief in the falsehood that vaccines cause autism. But at the same time, the message had an unexpected negative effect, decreasing the percentage of parents saying that they would be likely to vaccinate their children.

Looking more closely, the researchers found that this occurred because of a strong backfire effect among the minority of test subjects who were the most distrustful of vaccines. In this group, the likelihood of saying they would give their kids the MMR vaccine decreased to 45 percent (versus 70 percent in the control group) after they received factual, scientific information debunking the vaccines-autism link. Indeed, the study therefore concluded that "no intervention increased intent to vaccinate among parents who are the least favorable toward vaccines."

Nyhan carefully emphasizes that the study cannot say anything about the effectiveness of other possible messages beyond the ones that were tested. So there may be winners out there that simply weren't in the experiment—although as Nyhan added, "I don't have a good candidate." In any event, given results like these, any new messages ought to be tested as well.

"I don't think our results imply that they shouldn't communicate why vaccines are a good idea," adds Nyhan. "But they do suggest that we should be more careful to test the messages that we use, and to question the intuition that countering misinformation is likely to be the most effective strategy."

Finally, Nyhan adds that in order to protect public health by encouraging widespread vaccinations, public communication efforts aren't the only tools at our disposal. "Other policy measures might be more effective," he notes. For instance, recently we reported on how easy it is for parents to dodge getting their kids vaccinated in some states; in some cases, it requires little more than a onetime signature on a form. Tightening these policies might be considerably more helpful than trying to win hearts and minds. That wasn't really working out anyway, and thanks to the new study, we now know that vaccine deniers' imperviousness to facts may be a key part of the reason why.

Tighter Immigration Vaccination Policies Are Needed

Edith N. Nyangoma et al.

The following viewpoint was written by Edith N. Nyangoma and sixteen other authors. Nyangoma is an epidemic intelligence service officer at the Centers for Disease Control and Prevention.

On July 5, 2013, CDC [Centers for Disease Control and Prevention] was notified of two cases of laboratory-confirmed measles in recently adopted children from an orphanage in Henan Province, China. To find potentially exposed persons, CDC collaborated with state and local health departments, the children's adoption agency, and airlines that carried the adoptees. Two additional measles cases were identified, one in a family member of an adoptee and one in a third adopted child from China. To prevent further importation of measles, CDC worked with health officials in China, including "panel physicians" contracted by the U.S. Department of State to conduct the overseas medical examinations required for all immigrants and refugees bound for the United States. The following measures were recommended: 1) all adoptees examined at panel physician facilities should be screened for fever and rash illness, 2) measles immunity should be ensured among all adoptees from Henan Province who are scheduled for imminent departure to the United States, and 3) all children at the orphanage in Henan Province should be evaluated for measles. This report summarizes the results of the outbreak investigation and underscores the importance of timely routine vaccination for all international adoptees.

Edith N. Nyangoma et al., "Measles Outbreak Associated with Adopted Children from China—Missouri, Minnesota, and Washington," Centers for Disease Control and Prevention, July 2013.

Investigation and Public Health Response

A boy and a girl, both aged 2 years and with cerebral palsy, were in the process of being adopted by families in the United States, but became ill in China before traveling to the United States. The boy (child A) developed rhinorrhea and cough on June 24. At the time of his immigration medical examination by a panel physician on June 29, the boy was found to have a rash on his neck. Because he was afebrile [not feverish] and had no other symptoms or signs, the rash was diagnosed as contact dermatitis. By the next day, the rash began on his head and spread to his trunk and extremities, and he developed a fever. The girl (child B) was noted to be febrile on June 29 during her immigration medical examination, but no other symptoms or signs were present. Two days later, the panel physician was told by her adoptive parents that the girl was afebrile and doing well. However, investigators later learned that on June 29 the girl had developed cough, fever, and conjunctivitis, and on July 1 she had developed a rash on her face and neck.

Of 132 persons contacted, six were found to be susceptible to measles; three received postexposure immunoglobulin.

On July 4, both ill children traveled on different flights to the United States. They were hospitalized shortly after arrival in Washington and Missouri, respectively. Measles was confirmed in both children by positive immunoglobulin M (IgM) serology and polymerase chain reaction (PCR), and both were placed on isolation precautions. Neither child had documented measles vaccination, and their adoptive parents had executed affidavits, consistent with current policy, for exemption from the vaccine requirements for immigration until after their arrival in the United States.

State public health authorities notified CDC's Division of Global Migration and Quarantine (DGMQ) because both children were contagious during travel. DGMQ, working with U.S. Customs and Border Protection, obtained passenger and crew manifests and contact information from the airlines to investigate potential exposure of persons on flights with the ill children. A total of 83 crew members and passengers (those seated in the same row, two rows in front of, and two rows behind the ill children; infants in arms seated anywhere on either plane; and crew members who served passengers in the same cabin as either ill child) were identified as potentially exposed to measles. Contact information was available for 74 passengers and crew members from 20 states. Of the 29 passengers for whom follow-up data were available, two were found to be susceptible to measles, and one received postexposure immunoglobulin. No secondary measles cases associated with these flights were reported to CDC.

Local health officials conducted contact investigations with family members of the two ill adopted children, health-care personnel and other persons in health facilities where the children were treated, and two other U.S. families of recently adopted children who were in contact with the ill children in China. Contacts were interviewed about their travel history, presence of fever and rash, and measles immunity, either through documented vaccination or serologic tests. Contacts with no evidence of measles immunity were recommended to receive either postexposure vaccination with measles, mumps, and rubella (MMR) vaccine within 3 days of initial measles exposure or immunoglobulin administration within 6 days of initial measles exposure. Of 132 persons contacted, six were found to be susceptible to measles; three received postexposure immunoglobulin.

Two additional cases of measles were identified. Child C, aged 2 years in Minnesota, was adopted from China at the same time as child A and child B. Although child C was adopted from a different orphanage and traveled on different flights, he was exposed to the two infected children during the emigration process in China. Child C was asymptomatic and not contagious during travel. He arrived in the United States on July 4, developed a fever on July 10, rash on July 14, and tested IgM-positive for measles on July 16. This child also had cerebral palsy and no documentation of measles vaccination. The child's family members were fully immunized, and no secondary cases were reported.

Adoption of children from countries with high rates of vaccine-preventable diseases presents a challenge to the control of communicable diseases in the United States.

A fourth case was identified in the adoptive mother, aged 39 years, of child B. Although she reported a history of vaccination against measles, she developed signs and symptoms compatible with modified measles. On July 14 (2 weeks after symptom onset in child B), she developed a rash on her face and neck that lasted 4 days, but she had no fever, respiratory, or ocular symptoms. PCR and IgM tests performed on July 19 were positive for measles. An investigation of 19 contacts in this family revealed no additional cases.

Measles Outbreaks

Although endemic measles was declared eliminated from the United States in 2000, sporadic outbreaks still occur as a result of importations from areas where measles is endemic (1). Recent reported outbreaks have been associated with international adoptions, including two outbreaks among adoptees from China in 2004 and 2006. This report documents a cluster of imported measles cases among adoptees from China in July 2013.

China is the leading country of origin for internationally adopted children in the United States, contributing 30%

(2,696) of foreign-born adoptions in 2012. Through improved surveillance and enhanced nationwide vaccination campaigns using a 2-dose routine measles immunization schedule administered at 8 months and 18 months, with >90% measles vaccination coverage, cases of measles have significantly declined in China, from 2.8 per 100,000 in 2010 to 0.5 per 100,000 in 2012. However, in the first months of 2013, the number of measles cases in China rose to an incidence of 2.7 per 100,000.

Adoption of children from countries with high rates of vaccine-preventable diseases presents a challenge to the control of communicable diseases in the United States. Since 1996, the U.S. Department of State has required all persons seeking a U.S. immigrant visa to show proof of vaccination for certain vaccine-preventable diseases, including measles. However, internationally adopted children aged ≤10 years are exempted from this requirement if the adopting parent(s) sign an affidavit indicating that the child will receive vaccination within 30 days of entry into the United States. A significant public health risk is posed before, during, and after travel to the United States when parents choose not to vaccinate their children before leaving the country of origin. Children who are malnourished or have concomitant conditions, which are common among foreign-born adoptees, are especially vulnerable to severe forms of vaccine-preventable diseases. Parents who choose to sign the affidavit should ensure that adoptees receive age-appropriate vaccines, as recommended by the Advisory Committee on Immunization Practices, as soon as possible following entry into the United States.

Stronger Controls Needed

In this outbreak, all measles cases among adoptees were in unvaccinated children aged 2 years with cerebral palsy. Previous studies have shown that children with cerebral palsy are at risk for incomplete or delayed immunization, possibly as a result of the misconception that the MMR vaccine is associated with harmful neurologic side effects. Cerebral palsy is not a contraindication for MMR vaccination. Health-care providers should ensure that all children, including those with cerebral palsy, receive timely, age-appropriate routine immunizations, as recommended by the World Health Organization and the country of origin, unless contraindicated by medical conditions (e.g., history of anaphylactic reaction to a vaccine component).

Two of the ill children reported in this cluster were symptomatic and contagious en route to the United States, potentially exposing their families, many travelers, and hospital patients and staff members to measles. Had they been identified as infectious with measles before travel and prevented from boarding, subsequent contact investigations by health officials and the substantial costs associated with control of the outbreak could have been avoided. More importantly, routine vaccinations according to recommended schedules likely would have averted this outbreak. Public health and adoption agencies should continue to promote appropriate vaccinations for adoptees and their adoptive families

Anti-Vaxxers Should Have the Right to Choose Not to Vaccinate

Jeffrey A. Singer

Jeffrey A. Singer is a surgeon and an adjunct scholar at the Cato Institute.

In Steven Spielberg's 2002 sci-fi film *Minority Report*, a special police agency called PreCrime nabs suspects before they ever commit an offense. No trial is necessary because the crime is seen as an infallible prediction of the future and thus a matter of fact. The movie challenges viewers to consider the tension between technological determinism and free will, between the rights of an individual and the health of a community. It's a useful metaphor for the argument against coercive vaccination.

We Don't Know the Future

Some argue that mandatory mass vaccination is an act of communal self-defense, and thus completely compatible with the principles underpinning a free society. Unless people are forcibly immunized, they will endanger the life and health of innocent bystanders, goes the argument. But such a position requires a level of precognition we haven't yet attained.

Not everyone who is vaccinated against a microbe develops immunity to that microbe. Conversely, some unvaccinated people never become infected. Some people have inborn "natural" immunity against certain viruses and other microorganisms. Central Africans born with the sickle-cell trait provide a classic example of such inborn immunity: Their sickle-shaped red blood cells are inhospitable to the mosquito-borne parasite that causes malaria. Other people are just lucky and never get exposed to a contagious microbe.

Just like not every pregnant woman who drinks alcohol or smokes tobacco passes on a malady or disability to her newborn baby, not every pregnant woman infected with a virus or other microbe passes on the infection to her fetus—nor are all such babies born with birth defects.

How can defending forced immunization as self-defense be justified when it can never be shown with certainty that the non-vaccinated person would have been responsible for another person's harm?

A free society demands adherence to the non-aggression principle. No person should initiate force against another, and should only use force in retaliation or self-defense. Forcibly injecting substances—attenuated microbes or otherwise—into someone else's body cannot be justified as an act of self-defense, because there is no way to determine with certainty that the person will ever be responsible for disease transmission.

Ronald Bailey suggests that the choice to remain unvaccinated is analogous to "walking down a street randomly swinging your fists without warning." But this is a poor analogy. Such a person is engaging in a deliberate action, as opposed to choosing inaction. And, unlike those prevented from opting out of vaccination, the fist-swinger incurs no threat to life or limb when prohibited from throwing his punches.

Vaccination as Aggression

If someone chooses the inaction of non-vaccination based upon the belief—right or wrong—that the vaccination is harmful or even life threatening, then coercive vaccination in this context is clearly a case of aggression. For it to be otherwise requires certainty that those beliefs are wrong. And certainty in this case is not possible. How can you be sure, for example, that a child won't have an adverse or even fatal reaction to a vaccine? And how can defending forced immunization as self-defense be justified when it can never be shown with certainty that the non-vaccinated person would have been responsible for another person's harm?

Then there is the matter of "herd immunity." The phenomenon of herd immunity allows many unvaccinated people to avoid disease because they free ride off the significant portion of the population that is immunized. Economists point out that free riding is an unavoidable fact of life: People free ride when they purchase a new, improved, and cheaper product that was "pre-tested" on more affluent people who wanted to be the first to own it; people free ride when they use word-of-mouth reviews to decide whether to buy goods or services, or to see a film; those who choose not to carry concealed weapons free ride a degree of personal safety off the small percentage of the public that does.

So here is a way of thinking about it: As long as the person who is *being* free-ridden is still getting desired value for an acceptable price, and is not being harmed by the free riding, it really shouldn't matter. Achieving a society without free riders is not only unnecessary, it is impossible.

Even with the government school monopoly in existence today, immunization policy in at least 19 states is compatible with the non-aggression principle.

Perhaps allowing a certain number of free riders could mitigate the disruption to liberty caused by mandatory vaccination programs. But then, how many free riders should be allowed? I don't think that question can be answered with any degree of certainty. And what criteria would be used to decide who gets to ride free? An objective answer to this question appears equally elusive. Finally, how can the population be monitored to make sure the proportion of free riders is maintained at the right level without unreasonably infringing on civil liberties and privacy rights? The task would be titanic. I think the only practical solution—and the solution that is in the best interest of liberty—is to just accept the free riding of the current regime as a fact of reality, and focus instead on persuading people about the benefits of vaccination.

Most states coax, but don't coerce, vaccination of children in the public school system. Two of the 50 states, Mississippi and West Virginia, are indeed coercive. But the remaining 48 allow parents to opt out for religious reasons, and 19 allow for some kind of philosophical objection. Some states require parents to read about the risks of opting out before exempting their children. Some require them to acknowledge in writing that, in the event of a major school outbreak of a contagious disease for which their child has not received immunization, he or she will be held out of school until the outbreak clears.

Private schools requiring vaccination of children as a precondition for admission is not coercive, since private education is a voluntary transaction. But even with the government school monopoly in existence today, immunization policy in at least 19 states is compatible with the non-aggression principle.

Freedom Means Bad Choices

As a medical doctor I am a strong advocate of vaccination against communicable and infectious diseases. I am irritated by the hysteria and pseudo-science behind much of the anti-vaccination literature and rhetoric. In my perfect world, everyone would agree with me and voluntarily get vaccinated against the gamut of nasty diseases for which we have vaccines. (In my perfect world, pregnant women also wouldn't smoke tobacco or drink alcohol until after delivery.)

But free societies are sometimes messy. To live in a free society, one must be willing to tolerate people who make bad decisions and bad choices, as long as they don't directly infringe on the rights of others.

A strong argument can be made that it is self-defense to quarantine people who are infected with a disease-producing organism and are objectively threatening the contamination of others. But in such a case, the use of force against the disease carrier is based upon evidence that the carrier is contagious and may infect others.

Any mass immunization program that uses compulsion rather than persuasion will, on balance, do more harm to the well being of a free people than any good it was intended to convey.

Education Can Convince Parents to Vaccinate

Cochrane Community

The Cochrane Community is a global independent network of health practitioners, researchers, patient advocates, and others who work to produce credible, accessible information and research on health.

Vaccination has been described as one of the greatest public health achievements of the 20th century, and is a highly cost-effective public health measure. Childhood vaccinations can prevent illness and death from a variety of communicable diseases; despite this, many children do not get vaccinated. There are a number of reasons for this, including lack of knowledge about vaccine-preventable diseases, vaccinations, and where to access health services as well as poor access to vaccination services. People may also have concerns, or may be misinformed, about the benefits and harms of different vaccines, and as a result may refuse some or all vaccination of their children.

Communicate to Vaccinate

While access to vaccination is a key factor in many low- and middle-income country settings, vaccination refusal is an important issue in some settings and may have a significant impact on regional coverage. The term 'vaccine hesitancy' has been used in recent years to help define and understand behaviours relevant to vaccination decision making. The WHO [World Health Organization] defines vaccine-hesitant people as "a heterogeneous group who hold varying degrees of indecision about specific vaccines or vaccination in general."

Successful vaccination programmes rely on ensuring that participants have sufficient knowledge to make an informed decision to participate. In order to inform decisions and improve vaccination uptake, providers employ a range of strategies to communicate relevant information about child vaccination programmes to parents, caregivers, and communities. These strategies include interventions in which information is aimed at larger groups in the community, for instance at public meetings, through radio or through leaflets.

A team of Cochrane authors, based in Norway and South Africa and working with the Cochrane Consumers and Communication Group, set out to assess the effects of interventions aimed at communities to inform or educate people about vaccination in children aged six years and younger.

The trials show low-certainty evidence that interventions aimed at communities to inform and educate about childhood vaccination may improve knowledge of vaccines or vaccine-preventable diseases among intervention participants.

This Cochrane Review was undertaken as part of a larger research project called "Communicate to Vaccinate 1". This initiative focuses on building research knowledge and capacity to use evidence-based strategies to improve communication about childhood vaccinations with parents and communities in low- and middle-income countries (LMICs). The review is one of two focusing on communication interventions to inform and/or educate about childhood vaccination. The companion review focuses on face-to-face interventions for informing or educating parents, and the two reviews were developed in close collaboration.

Interventions aimed at communities or community members are used widely, but the implementation of such programmes requires resources including money, time, and trained personnel. The research team therefore felt it was critical to determine whether these interventions are effective, so as to inform decisions about the use of finite, and usually limited, resources within vaccination programmes.

Some Increase on Vaccinations

The Cochrane authors identified two cluster-randomised trials that compared interventions aimed at communities to routine immunisation practices. In one study, from India, families, teachers, children and village leaders were encouraged to attend information meetings, where they received information about childhood vaccination and could ask questions. In the other study, from Pakistan, people who were considered to be trusted in the community were invited to meetings to discuss vaccine coverage rates in their community, as well as the costs and benefits of childhood vaccination. They were asked to develop local action plans, to share the information that they had been given, and to continue the discussions in their communities.

The trials show low-certainty evidence that interventions aimed at communities to inform and educate about childhood vaccination may improve knowledge of vaccines or vaccine-preventable diseases among intervention participants. There is also low-certainty evidence that these interventions may change attitudes in favour of vaccination among parents with young children. In addition, there is moderate-certainty evidence that these interventions probably increase the number of children who get vaccinated.

The review provides limited evidence to inform decisions regarding the implementation of this type of community-aimed intervention. Some of these interventions may be resource intensive when implemented in a larger population, and therefore the decision to develop them and to allocate resources for implementation, may need to be made with caution and be targeted to where the interventions have the potential to provide greatest benefit. However, it is also important to consider that interventions aimed at communities may be cost-effective in some settings even if these interventions result in small increases in vaccination uptake, as the costs of non-vaccination are likely to be very high.

"The findings of this review must be considered alongside other relevant reviews in order to understand the best mix of interventions in different settings," said Ingvil Saeterdal, a researcher at the Norwegian Knowledge Centre for the Health Services and lead author of the Cochrane Review. "Interventions aimed at communities should be implemented in the context of rigorous evaluation, to continue to build the evidence base in this area of practice."

Forget "Anti-Vaxxers." The Disney Measles Outbreak Could Change the Minds of a More Crucial Group

Todd C. Frankel

Todd C. Frankel is a reporter covering people and policy for The Washington Post.

The child was behind on her vaccinations. Wendy Sue Swanson took note of this as she talked with the girl's parents last week at a medical clinic in Mill Creek, Wash., outside Seattle.

Disney Outbreak Changes Minds

Swanson, like many pediatricians, sometimes needed to coax parents to get the shots for their children. A few might be unmovable in their objections. But most were like this couple: A mom and dad who might harbor doubts or were just behind schedule. They were at least willing to listen.

Now, Swanson had a new way to prod parents like them: Discussing the Disney measles outbreak in California, which has spread to at least 68 people in 11 states since Jan. 1 [2015] and raised alarms about the reemergence of a disease once considered all but vanquished. There was something powerful about the disease hitting a popular, recognizable vacation spot.

The girl got her vaccination. Her parents were on board.

"Their eagerness was different," Swanson said later. "I think it is changing people."

Much of the scrutiny in the Disney measles outbreak has fallen on an entrenched anti-vaccination movement in places such as Orange County, Calif., home to the two Disney theme parks where the outbreak gained its foothold. These "anti-vaxxers" are viewed as dead-set against vaccinations.

But doctors believe the current outbreak could change the minds of a less-known but even larger group: parents who remain on the fence about the shots. These "vaccine-hesitant" parents have some doubt about vaccinations, leading them to question or skip some shots, stagger their delivery or delay them beyond the recommended schedule. An estimated 5 to 11 percent of U.S. parents have skipped at least one vaccination or delayed a shot, according to studies. That compares to only 1 to 3 percent of parents who object to all vaccinations.

One of the problems that vaccines face now is they work too well.

Boosting compliance among the "vaccine hesitant" population could have major public health implications, doctors say, especially because last year the United States had its highest number of measles cases since 1977. The topic of "vaccine hesitant" patients has become the focus of a growing body of medical research in recent years. Doctors are trying to understand what triggers vaccine worries and which strategies work best for overcoming those fears.

Doctors spend many office hours trying to convince these parents that the scientific evidence proves the shots are in fact safe and effective. But these hesitant parents have been bombarded by conflicting information. And they don't view all of the shots the same way. The vaccine to protect against measles, mumps and rubella faces particularly strong resistance as a result of thoroughly discredited studies linking the vaccine to autism. So some parents, even those generally open to other vaccines, push to delay or skip this one. The shot is supposed to be given at 12 months and again at age 4.

"One of the problems that vaccines face now is they work too well," said Michael Smith, a pediatric infectious disease specialist at the University of Louisville School of Medicine in Kentucky, who has studied vaccine-hesitant parents.

Parents don't have experience with measles, how children can become very ill and in rare cases suffer brain swelling or even die, Smith said. At the same time, these parents are confronted with stories about the unexplained rise in the U.S. autism rate.

"I can understand as a parent why you'd skip the vaccine if you'd been convinced that it's a choice between giving my kids a shot or giving my kid autism," Smith said.

Concrete Threat

But the Disney outbreak changes the discussion. Now, doctors have an event to point to. The threat is no longer abstract or distant.

"This is definitely going to be a talking point that pediatricians should keep in their back pockets," Smith said.

Studies have shown that "anti-vaxxer" parents are likely to remain steadfast in their opposition. Barbara Loe Fisher, president of the National Vaccine Information Center, a group that raises doubts about the shots, said she was not convinced that the Disney outbreak was even a story about the dangers of being unvaccinated.

I don't think we know completely what's going on, Fisher said.

But physicians such as Kathryn Edwards of the Vanderbilt Vaccine Research Program said the measles vaccine is at least 99 percent effective after the second dose. And measles is one of the most communicable diseases, much more so than the flu. The dangers posed by the disease have been forgotten.

Many U.S. doctors have never even seen it. Edwards still recalls the only patient she ever saw with measles, years ago when she was a medical resident. He died.

"So I have a lot of respect for measles," Edwards said.

At Boston Children's Hospital, pediatrician Claire McCarthy said she is always happy when parents decide to vaccinate their children against measles in particular. She worries about the current situation in California. And she plans to use the Disney outbreak to try to convince hesitant parents that vaccinations are the right choice.

"I am planning on talking this one up a lot with families," McCarthy said. "I think this probably will make a difference."

Fear of Unvaccinated Immigrants Is Overblown

Rachel Pearson

Rachel Pearson is a medical and PhD student at the Institute for the Medical Humanities and the University of Texas Medical Branch.

With thousands of children from Central America arriving at the U.S.-Mexico border, an old plague is once again sweeping the country—the fear of the diseased immigrant.

False Fears of Diseased Immigrants

"Our schools cannot handle this influx, we don't even know what all diseases they have," U.S. Rep. Louie Gohmert (R-TX) said recently. "Our health care systems can't withstand this influx."

Fox News commentator Cal Thomas asks, for example, if "the unaccompanied minors pouring over the border . . . have brought with them proof of vaccination?" Thomas accuses the border-crossers of harboring vaccine-preventable diseases such as "mumps, measles, rubella, polio, tetanus and diphtheria."

Before demonizing undocumented children, we should look at the facts: The vast majority of Central Americans are vaccinated against all these diseases. Governments concerned about health, and good parents investing in their kids, have made Central American kids better-vaccinated than Texan kids. We fear them not because they are actually sick, but because of powerful anti-immigration narratives that link foreigners to disease.

Consider, for example, Guatemala. According to the United Nations Children's Fund (UNICEF), Guatemalan kids are more likely than Texans to be immunized for most infectious diseases. Guatemala has universal health care. Vaccines are 100 percent funded by the government.

By comparison, one in six kids in Texas is uninsured, and even insured families often must pay for vaccination. That means that many Texas kids fall behind on vaccinations, or miss them altogether when their family can't afford a doctor's visit. Other families refuse vaccination.

It's absurd to claim that the U.S. has eradicated measles while Central America has not. In fact, measles outbreaks have resurged in some American cities.

Dr. Elizabeth Lee Vliet, a Fox News commentator and former director of the ultra-conservative political group Association of American Physicians and Surgeons, writes in the McAllen *Monitor* that measles is among the "diseases the United States had controlled or virtually eradicated" that are "carried across the border by this tsunami of illegals."

Fact check: UNICEF reports that 93 percent of kids in Guatemala, Honduras and El Salvador are vaccinated against measles. That's better than American kids (92 percent).

Furthermore, it's absurd to claim that the U.S. has eradicated measles while Central America has not. In fact, measles outbreaks have resurged in some American cities. By contrast, according to the World Health Organization, neither Guatemala nor Honduras has had a reported case of measles since 1990.

Slate physician-writer (and Fox News contributor) Marc Siegel writes that unaccompanied minors "are a likely source" of the mosquito-borne dengue fever spreading to Texas. Siegel ignores two key public health points: First, legal immigrants and travelers are a much larger group than undocumented folks, and just as likely to carry dengue. (I don't know about y'all, but I've never been screened for dengue fever at the Texas-Mexico border.) Second, mosquitoes can fly.

Interestingly, Siegel is the author of three books—*Swine Flu: The New Pandemic, Bird Flu: Everything You Need to Know About the Next Pandemic* and *False Alarm: Profiting from the Epidemic of Fear.* That last title must be a memoir.

The narrative that foreigners bring disease has long been used to stir up anti-immigrant sentiment. In the early 1900s, the immigrant cook Mary Mallon—better known as Typhoid Mary—was imprisoned for life for infecting her wealthy patrons with Salmonella *typhii.*

The targeting of vulnerable outsiders whenever disease breaks out is even older than this country.

In his book *The Cholera Years,* historian Charles Rosenberg describes how Irish immigrants to New York in the 1830s suffered disproportionately from cholera because they lived in poor and crowded neighborhoods. Instead of working to help them, the medical profession blamed the disease on immigrants being "exceedingly dirty." Irish people were refused medical care, and many "wandered starved and half naked across the Canadian border."

When Hurricane Katrina devastated New Orleans in 2005, the Latino men who came to work rebuilding the city were accused of spreading infectious diseases such as chlamydia and HIV.

The targeting of vulnerable outsiders whenever disease breaks out is even older than this country. Historian Barbara Tuchman has described how outbreaks of plague in Europe would lead to pogroms. The lynchings of Jews, she writes "began in 1348 on the heels of the first plague deaths." When we blame immigrants for infectious disease, we participate in a nasty—and deadly—old tradition.

Immigrants Are Not to Blame

Some diseases do flourish because of unsanitary conditions in the immigrant detention centers. For example, Fox News reports that the Border Patrol union is complaining that an agent "already has contracted the mite-borne skin infection" scabies. Like lice, scabies is annoying but eminently treatable. It spreads anywhere people are in close quarters: summer camps, homeless shelters, college dorms.

While outbreaks of scabies are a decent indicator that conditions in the detention centers are unsanitary, scabies is not the kind of disease that should dictate immigration policy. To get rid of it, you treat the kid and wash his or her bedding.

Tuberculosis (TB) is one of the diseases most calculated to frighten Texans. On the right-wing blog Breitbart Texas, Vliet claims that immigrants with TB "are putting others' lives at risk," and that multi-drug-resistant TB is the "most common form" of TB in Latin America.

The latter is simply false: Fewer than 1 percent of TB cases in the Americas are multi-drug-resistant, according to the WHO [World Health Organization]. Most of those cases are still treatable. According to the Texas Department of State Health Services (DSHS), no cases of the more difficult extensively drug-resistant TB (XDR-TB) were reported here in 2012.

Fear of disease is motivating people to move against immigrants.

More than 90 percent of Central Americans are vaccinated against TB, according to the WHO. The vaccine, called the BCG, is imperfect. It's used in countries where TB is still common, but some cases will break through the vaccine's coverage.

Americans are not routinely vaccinated. According to the state health department, the 1,233 cases of TB that occurred in Texas in 2012 were mostly along the border and in prisons.

The disease has stayed crouched in those centers of poverty because it flourishes where people live in close quarters and suffer from diseases like alcoholism and HIV, which knock down their immune defenses. Eradicate poverty, and TB fades away.

Fear of disease is motivating people to move against immigrants. In League City, the City Council voted this week to prohibit the housing or processing of undocumented immigrants. The resolution cited the "threat of communicable diseases reported to be prevalent" among immigrants as a justification for the use of police power to protect "citizens" from these children.

And in Murrieta, California, protesters blocked buses carrying migrant children after it was revealed that some of them had been hospitalized for fevers.

Fear turns sick kids into a threat. But the threat of tuberculosis is overblown. The state health department is screening unaccompanied minors for the disease. Some small percentage of them—like a tiny percentage of Texan kids overall—probably have TB. It can be controlled and treated before it spreads.

Even if these unaccompanied minors did pose a huge tuberculosis threat—which they do not—Texas is equipped to deal with it. We have clinics, first-line antibiotics and even a tuberculosis sanitarium to house folks who can't keep up with the daily antibiotics on their own.

There are legitimate health concerns associated with human migration. But the narrative that immigrants such as these children are particularly diseased has more to do with fear than it does with science.

CHAPTER 3

Does an HIV/AIDS Crisis Still Exist?

Chapter Preface

In the United States, HIV/AIDS is generally thought of as a disease in retreat. Understanding of the disease, antiretroviral drugs, and a strong health-care system have reduced both infections and deaths from AIDS over the last decades. But these victories over AIDS can be reversed—as a recent outbreak in Indiana has demonstrated.

Indiana has the lowest per person health-care spending of any state in the country. In recent years it has closed health centers for HIV testing, largely because these centers are run by Planned Parenthood, which provides reproductive care, including abortions, opposed by conservative leaders in Indiana's government. Similarly, Indiana has banned and eliminated programs that make clean syringes available to drug users, so that they don't have to share needles.

Add to all this a growth in heroin use, and the result is an AIDS crisis in the state. As of mid-April 2015, more than 130 cases of HIV had been reported in southeastern Indiana. Governor Mike Pence declared a state of emergency. Among other policies, he suspended the state ban on needle exchange programs, though only for thirty days and only in the worst affected area, Scott County. "In response to a public health emergency, I'm prepared to make an exception to my long-standing opposition to needle exchange programs," he said, but added, "I don't believe that effective anti-drug policy involves handing out paraphernalia to drug users by government officials."[1]

Pence's position seems conflicted. If needle exchange can reduce HIV infection in an emergency, it seems like a policy that the state would want to pursue in order to prevent a cri-

1. Quoted in Zoë Carpenter, "The Indiana HIV Crisis Didn't Have to Happen," *The Nation*, April 1, 2015. http://www.thenation.com/blog/203185/indiana-hiv-crisis-didnt -have-happen#.

sis in the first place. But it also demonstrates how political considerations and ideology can allow HIV/AIDS to regain a foothold in parts of the United States where it had been in decline. Ed Clere, a Republican state representative and chairman of the public health committee, has argued for expanded needle exchange programs. "The fact is that the situation could repeat itself anywhere else in Indiana at any time,"[2] he said. Underfunded health-care systems and political resistance to best health practices will fuel the spread of other diseases as well—the AIDS crisis in Indiana was actually preceded by a rash of cases of Hepatitis C. HIV/AIDs may be contained in much of the United States, but Indiana shows that it can quickly gain a foothold again.

The remainder of this chapter looks at other controversies about whether there is an ongoing HIV/AIDS crisis in the United States and in other regions of the world.

---

2. Quoted in Amanda Holpuch, "Indiana Health Workers Face HIV Outbreak 'with Two Hands Tied Behind Our Back,'" *Guardian*, April 1, 2015. http://www.theguardian.com /us-news/2015/apr/01/indiana-hiv-outbreak-health-workers-funding.

African Americans Face an Ongoing AIDS Crisis

Irene Monroe

Irene Monroe is a Huffington Post *blogger and a syndicated religion columnist.*

President [Barack] Obama conveyed hopeful remarks on World AIDS Day [December 1, 2014] at George Washington University (GWU) in D.C., vowing to continue efforts to combat the disease.

"We're closer than we've ever been to achieving the extraordinary: an AIDS-free generation," Obama stated to the GWU audience. "But we've got to keep fighting, all of us—governments, businesses, foundations, community groups, and individuals like you."

AIDS in Washington, D.C.

In 2012, the United Nations stated that it's possible to eradicate the disease by 2015—in part, of course, by preventing new infections.

But much of the focus was, and still is, on developing countries, and not on hotspots like the nation's capital, which is one of the hardest hit areas battling the epidemic.

In 2006, at the "Women and Response to AIDS" panel at the conference, Sheila Johnson, founder of the Crump-Johnson Foundation in Washington D.C., pointed out that another at-risk population in the African-American community is teen-age girls.

Seventeen percent of the U.S. teen population is African American, but African Americans make up 70 percent of HIV-positive teens. One in 10 black teenage girls test HIV-positive in the nation's capital, the highest percentage in the country among this age group.

When asked why such a high percentage test positive, Johnson said, "As long as girls see themselves as glorified sex objects in hip-hop videos, HIV/AIDS will increase within this population." In 2014 little has changed within this demographic group.

Each year, fewer and fewer public events are being held to bring public attention that the [AIDS] epidemic is still in our midst.

And sadly, with African Americans being infected with the AIDS virus at younger and younger ages, the life expectancy rate of African Americans will decline. Soon we will no longer expect today's young African-Americans to become the elders of the community.

AIDS in the South

With the South's propensity to avoid speaking about uncomfortable subjects, that region has unfortunately evolved into one of the country's HIV/AIDS hotspots.

Each year, fewer and fewer public events are being held to bring public attention that the epidemic is still in our midst. This year, PBS's *Frontline* didn't run its special "Endgame: AIDS in Black America."

With the latest comprehensive data tracking the virus coming out of the Centers for Disease Control [and Prevention] (CDC) the numbers are staggeringly alarming.

Although African Americans now comprise nearly 13 percent of the U.S. population, we tragically account for approximately 44 percent of new HIV infections in 2010.

But this data doesn't reflect the wave of recent African diasporic immigrants of the last decade coming from the Caribbean Islands and the Motherland. This demographic group is overwhelmingly underreported and underserved—for fear of not only deportation but also of homophobic insults and assaults from their communities.

According to the CDC in 2010, 1 in 22 African Americans will be diagnosed HIV-positive in their lifetime. And it's the leading cause of death among African American women between the ages of 25–34 and African American men between the ages of 35–44.

The good news is that HIV infections among African American women only in Massachusetts has decreased for the first time. And this decline in numbers has much to do with the indefatigable outreach by local organizations like AIDS Action Committee, which are operating on state grants that diminish each year.

According to the Black AIDS Institute's August 2008 report, "Left Behind," the number of people living with HIV in black America exceeds the HIV population in seven of the fifteen focus countries in the U.S. President's Emergency Plan for AIDS Relief (PEPFAR) initiative, a program to save the lives of those suffering from HIV/AIDS around the world in countries like Haiti, Dominican Republic, India, South Africa.

While we know that the epidemic moves along the fault lines of race, class, gender, and sexual orientation . . . homophobia still continues to be one of the major barriers to ending the AIDS epidemic.

In other words, if black America were its own country, standing on its own like Haiti or Nigeria, black Americans would rate 16th with the epidemic in the world. The epidemic is heavily concentrated in urban enclaves like Detroit; New York; Newark; Washington, D.C.; and the Deep South.

There are many persistent social and economic factors contributing to the high rates of the epidemic in the African

American community—racism, poverty, health care disparity, violence, to name just a few—but the biggest attitudinal factor still contributing to the epidemic (and showing no sign of abating) is homophobia.

While we know that the epidemic moves along the fault lines of race, class, gender, and sexual orientation—and that HIV transmission is tied to specific high-risk behaviors that are not exclusive to any one sexual orientation—homophobia still continues to be one of the major barriers to ending the AIDS epidemic.

Famous HIV-positive heterosexual African Americans like tennis great Arthur Ashe, news anchorman Max Robinson, and rapper Eazy all died of AIDS, and basketball giant Earvin "Magic" Johnson, who is still living with the virus, highlight the fact that anyone can contract the virus, but many still see the epidemic as a "white gay disease," suggesting being gay or having sex with someone of the same gender puts you immediately at high risk.

But the truth is this: while over 600,000 African Americans are now living with HIV and as many 30,000 are newly infected each year, there is still within the black community at least one in five people living with HIV and unaware of their infection—and they are disproportionately heterosexuals.

While the number of cases across the globe will continue to decline and possibly eradicate the disease as the U.N. [United Nations] hopefully predicts, we as African Americans will not be able to protect ourselves from this epidemic as long as we continue to think of HIV/AIDS as a "gay disease."

China Continues to Struggle with Its AIDS Crisis

Malcolm Moore

Malcolm Moore is the Beijing correspondent for The Telegraph.

At first, he did not know he was sick. He went back to school but complained of "month-long" fevers and some mornings he found he could not even open his eyes. After leaving school, he worked in factories and then dug irrigation systems in western China.

Now aged 28, Mr Wang was diagnosed with full-blown Aids in May. "My parents cried for four days. I am their only son," he said, sitting inside a restaurant in Beijing but huddled in an overcoat with a fake-fur collar.

Nor is he the only victim. Between 50,000 and 300,000 others were also mistakenly infected with HIV in Mr Wang's home province of Henan in the 1990s, in one of the biggest medical scandals of all time.

There are no official figures because the Chinese government has never admitted or apologised for what happened. And the man who led the cover-up in Henan has just been anointed as China's new prime minister: Li Keqiang.

Now that Mr Li has reached the apex of power, he appears keen to fix the worst stain on his political career.

One of his first acts was to intervene on behalf of a 25-year-old HIV positive lung cancer patient who had been denied an operation in Tianjin.

Earlier this week [November 2012] Mr Li shook hands with Aids victims on Chinese television and promised to let

NGOs [nongovernmental organizations] play a more active role in battling the disease. China saw a 13 per cent rise in infections last year [2011].

Last Friday, following Mr Li's orders, the health ministry banned hospitals from turning away infected patients.

It was a step to calm the public anger in Henan, where 300 Aids victims tore down the gates of the local government in September to protest their lack of treatment.

The Aids epidemic broke out in Henan after local officials encouraged farmers to donate blood and failed to properly screen the process.

Mr Wang said his local hospital would not treat him for lesions he has developed on his liver because of his disease. Two of the three retroviral drugs he takes each morning are no longer used in the West because they can cause liver damage.

At the same time, Mr Wang said, the shadow of the virus still hangs over the health system. Even today, he said, "Chinese hospitals cannot guarantee that their blood is safe". The World Health Organisation declined to comment.

The Aids epidemic broke out in Henan after local officials encouraged farmers to donate blood and failed to properly screen the process.

"Extend your arm. Expose a vein. Make a fist. And it's 50 yuan (£5)" was a popular slogan, as mobile collection units hustled for blood. Needles were reused and, most chillingly, donors were reinjected with pooled blood once the plasma had been removed.

By 1996, when Mr Wang was infected, local officials were already aware that the province's blood banks were badly contaminated. But instead of raising the alert, they covered up the news and muzzled journalists and doctors.

"When I first found out, my first thought was to take re-venge, to suicide bomb the hospital. But then I thought there are other innocent patients there so I changed my mind," said Mr Wang.

Even today, almost 15 years since the scandal came to light, mobs of thugs patrol the worst-affected villages in Henan, closing them off to the outside world.

Since he was diagnosed, Mr Wang has lived alone in his village in Runan county. Around 100 others nearby were also infected by blood transfusions at Runan hospital.

No officials have ever been punished, but the doctor who performed Mr Wang's surgery has been transferred elsewhere, after a number of his patients became HIV positive.

"I take care of myself basically," he said. "I go to the hospi-tal in the morning for my medication on a scooter. It is about three miles away. My parents have gone to the south. They felt ashamed to stay in the village.

"I am alone all the time. I watch television day and night, I watch NBA basketball during the day. Everyone in the village knows I am a carrier and no one comes to see me anymore."

But he said many other victims have lost hope. "Probably about a third of them cannot get any compensation from the court and are taking their revenge by deliberately infecting others," he said. "I know at least ten people who are doing that."

"They cannot see a future and the government is not mak-ing them confident that they will live for a long time. They want to make the best of their remaining time and have fun. They should have justice and they should have jobs, but they are discriminated against," he added.

Because of the cover-up, many victims unwittingly in-fected their wives, or others. "I heard that in the Runan Nor-mal College a lot of female students were infected who were mistresses of local people," he said.

"One of the teachers also was infected, after sleeping with a student. The girls were quietly persuaded to leave class and many of them have gone to the south to work, some of them becoming prostitutes," he said.

The court in Runan awarded Mr Wang £6,000 in compensation but he is now fighting with the court system to compel his hospital to treat him. He came to Beijing to protest outside the Supreme Court. But upon trying to unfurl a red banner calling for justice, he was quickly ushered away by the guards outside.

Homophobia in Russia Is Fueling an AIDS Crisis

Hayato Watanabe

Hayato Watanabe is a graduate student in the department of politics at New York University.

The 2014 Winter Olympics in Sochi Russia ignited a conflict-ridden and violent discussion about the status of LGBT [lesbian, gay, bisexual, and transgender] rights in the country. News of hate crimes and protest crackdowns sparked a firestorm of outrage among international and local gay rights activists, who are calling for greater scrutiny of the [Vladimir] Putin administration. But the consequences of the LGBT struggle in Russia extend even beyond the violence seen on TV.

An Epidemic

The HIV/AIDS epidemic in Russia is spiraling out of control, and LGBT communities are some of the most seriously affected. From 2002 to 2012, the number of people living with HIV/AIDS in Russia has increased an astounding 41%, with the numbers of those infected towering over 1.3 million. The Putin administration is ignoring the needs of this community, and is worsening the epidemic by promoting laws that stigmatize homosexuality. Greater international attention must be brought to the relationship between Russia's homophobic politics and public health. The Russian government must be pushed towards more equitable policies on both LGBT and HIV/AIDS issues.

Recently, global infection statistics have declined in historically hard-hit areas such as India and South Africa. Sadly, this trend has not made it to Russia—the infection rate there has increased 7% just this year. These new HIV cases are a direct result of Russia's policies. They refuse adequate HIV/AIDS services, stop information about safe sex, and shun the LGBT community into fearing violence, or even death.

Russia has passed legislation that bans the "propaganda" of nontraditional sexual relations to minors. In reality, any sign of sexual nonconformity, at any age to any audience, is met with brutal repression. Gay rights activists have widely condemned the law since its passage in June 2013, but Russian officials have shown no intention of backing down from their hardline stance on gay rights.

Russia's [anti-gay propaganda] law reinforces the narrative that LGBT people are not deserving of respect and equality.

If Russian lawmakers cannot look to their own consciences on the issue of LGBT discrimination, maybe they will listen to statistics, or to the cries of the international [community] when the devastating consequences of this law are fully realized.

Fear, Shame and Health

Health activists are concerned that ratcheting up anti-LGBT rhetoric, in addition to fanning the flames of anti-LGBT hysteria, will impede the dissemination of accurate AIDS awareness information. This will affect the ability of health professionals to reach individuals who have been affected by HIV/AIDS or who might be at risk.

Russia's law reinforces the narrative that LGBT people are not deserving of respect and equality. By further engendering a culture of shame, the law may cause individuals seeking testing and treatment to conceal their homosexuality, or to falsely attribute their status to other methods of transmission (such as injection drug use), in order to avoid the stigma of being gay.

Misreporting or underreporting created by an environment of fear and shame constrains the ability of health professionals to properly study and address the HIV/AIDS crisis. Additionally, the conflation of HIV stigma and gay stigma may even stop heterosexual people from seeking testing. These policies obscure how many diverse communities grapple with this epidemic, and will have disastrous consequences down the line. Along with country's failure to address drug addiction that also spreads HIV/AIDS, Russia's stance on the LGBT community is repressive and backward.

Unfortunately, the outlook appears bleak. The ongoing conflict in Crimea has destabalized relations between Russia and the international community, diminishing hope that Russian lawmakers can be lobbied to repeal the anti-gay propaganda law or allocate more funds to battle the HIV/AIDS crisis.

While the world is obsessed with debating whether Russia's takeover of Crimea constitutes an act of war, Russia is waging another war—one against its own LGBT people. The Russian government is advancing a health agenda that neglects the needs of one of its most vulnerable communities and treats them like second-class citizens.

Russia needs to repair its approach to public health and its fractured relationship with its LGBT citizens. The country could start by repealing the anti-gay propaganda law. Ending stigma and inspiring openness will not only increase testing, it will also encourage greater awareness of HIV/AIDS related issues.

The Russian government must also ensure there are ample resources available to educate the public and help those grappling with HIV/AIDS. For example, the government could sponsor initiatives that provide access to accurate sex education. Accurate knowledge is the first critical step towards ending this global epidemic. The government should also subsidize medications such as post-exposure prophylaxis, which can actually prevent transmission in high-risk situations. Finally, ensuring that HIV positive people have access to medication is critical, because maintaining low viral loads can affect how easily the virus is spread.

Russia's anti-LGBT propaganda law is shameful—and it's also an example of shockingly bad policy. The government's intransigence on the issue of LGBT rights challenges the "it gets better" idealism trumpeted by the larger international gay rights movement. Rather, things seem to be moving backwards in Russia, impeding the country's ability to stop an epidemic. As some LGBT Russians might say, "it gets better everywhere but here."

The AIDS Epidemic Continues in Africa

AVERT

AVERT is an international AIDS charity.

South Africa has the biggest and most high profile HIV epidemic in the world, with an estimated 6.3 million people living with HIV in 2013. In the same year, there were 330,000 new infections while 200,000 South Africans died from AIDS-related illnesses.

South Africa has the largest antiretroviral treatment programme globally and these efforts have been largely financed from its own domestic resources. The country now invests more than $1 billion annually to run its HIV and AIDS programmes. However, HIV prevalence remains high (19.1%) among the general population, although it varies markedly between regions. For example, HIV prevalence is almost 40% in Kwazulu Natal compared with 18% in Northern Cape and Western Cape.

Key Affected Populations in South Africa. South Africa's National Strategic Plan 2012-2016 identifies a number of key affected populations that are at risk of HIV transmission.

Men Who Have Sex with Men (MSM)

HIV prevalence among men who have sex with men (MSM) in South Africa is an estimated 9.9% with roughly 9.2% of all new HIV infections among this group. HIV prevalence among MSM varies geographically. For example, one study reported an HIV prevalence of 43.6% among MSM in

AVERT, "HIV and AIDS in Sub-Saharan Africa," May 20, 2014. www.avert.org /professionals/hiv-around-world/sub-saharan-africa/south-africa. Copyright © 2015 AVERT. All rights reserved. Reproduced with permission.

Johannesburg and Durban. By contrast, 10% of self-identified MSM from urban areas in Western Cape are reportedly living with HIV.

Many MSM still face high levels of social stigma and homophobic violence due to traditional and conservative attitudes. A 2013 study found that only 32% of South Africans said that homosexuality should be accepted by society. As a result, MSM find it difficult to disclose their sexuality to healthcare workers, limiting their access to HIV services.

Educational organisations have reported difficulties in delivering HIV prevention services to sex workers due to on-going police harassment.

However, South Africa is the only country in sub-Saharan Africa where gay rights are formally recognised. Moreover, national policies strongly emphasise equity, social justice and forbid discrimination based on sexual orientation. These are prerequisites for the provision of HIV services for MSM as well as other members of the lesbian, gay, bisexual and transgender (LGBT) community. As a result, South Africa has the potential to provide a leading role in the improvement of HIV service provision for MSM throughout sub-Saharan Africa.

Sex Workers

HIV prevalence among sex workers varies between 34% and 69% depending on the geographical area. In 2010, sex work accounted for an estimated 19.8% of all new HIV infections in South Africa.

Sex workers in South Africa also face high levels of stigma and discrimination and are restricted by the laws under which they have to work. Moreover, many sex workers also inject drugs, exacerbating their vulnerability to HIV infection. Female sex workers (FSW) are particularly affected with one study reporting an HIV prevalence of nearly 60% among FSW compared to 13% among women in the general population.

Educational organisations have reported difficulties in delivering HIV prevention services to sex workers due to ongoing police harassment. One study found that up to 70% of women who sold sex had experienced abuse by the authorities:

> "He put me on the floor. The police officer raped me, then the second one, after that the third one did it again. I was crying after the three left without saying anything. Then the first one appeared again . . . He let me out by the back gate without my property. I was so scared that my family would find out."—Female sex worker, Cape Town

In light of this, the South African National AIDS Council (SANAC) recently commissioned the first ever study assessing the number of sex workers in the country. It is hoped that this report will enable South Africa to better estimate the need for HIV services among this group in order to develop effective policy.

People Who Inject Drugs (PWID)

Data on HIV prevalence among people who inject drugs (PWID) in South Africa is very limited and where it does exists, is based on small sample sizes. In 2012, an estimated 16.2% of PWID in South Africa were living with HIV. However, PWID account for a comparatively low 1.3% of new HIV infections.

There are . . . over 2.5 million children in South Africa who have been orphaned by HIV and AIDS.

One study has reported that up to 86% of South Africans who inject drugs share injection equipment such as syringes and other drug paraphernalia. Another study reported that some PWID re-use equipment between 2 and 15 times.

PWID are also associated with other high-risk behaviours such as sex work and unsafe sexual practices. For example, the

IRARE study demonstrated a strong link between drug use and risky sexual practices with up to 65% of PWID in South Africa thought to practice unsafe sex.

Children and Orphans

In 2012, an estimated 410,000 children aged 0 to 14 were living with HIV in South Africa. From 2002 to 2012, HIV prevalence declined among children, due mainly to programmes to prevent the mother-to-child transmission of HIV (PMTCT). The scaling up of antiretroviral treatment has reduced child mortality by 20%.

There are also over 2.5 million children in South Africa who have been orphaned by HIV and AIDS. Orphans are particularly vulnerable to HIV transmission; they are often at risk of being forced into sex, have sex in exchange for support, and typically become sexually active earlier than other children.

HIV prevalence among women aged 15-24 is thought to have declined between 2002 and 2012.

The National Strategic Plan 2012-2016 aims to lessen the impact of HIV on orphans, vulnerable children and youth by ensuring they have access to vital social services, including basic education.

Women

An HIV survey in 2012 found that HIV prevalence among women was nearly twice that in men. Rates of new infections among young women aged 15-24 were more than four times greater than that of men in the same age range, and accounted for 25% of new infections in South Africa.

Studies have shown how due to the high numbers of HIV-positive men compared to women in South Africa, HIV transmission rates from men to women have increased. Poverty, the low status of women and gender-based violence have also been cited as reasons for the disparity in HIV prevalence between men and women in South Africa.

Despite these barriers, HIV prevalence among women aged 15-24 is thought to have declined between 2002 and 2012. . . .

HIV and Tuberculosis (TB) in South Africa. South Africa also has the world's third largest tuberculosis (TB) epidemic. The HIV epidemic in South Africa fuels the TB epidemic as people living with HIV are at a far higher risk of developing TB as a weakened immune system allows the development of the disease. 70% of people living with HIV in South Africa are also co-infected with TB.

However, the TB cure rate has improved in recent years. Between 2010 and 2011, the number of people living with HIV who received TB treatment nearly tripled, from 146,000 in 2010 to 373,000 in 2011.

> "We cannot fight AIDS unless we do much more to fight TB."—Nelson Mandela

---

South Africa has made great strides in tackling its HIV epidemic in recent years.

HIV Funding in South Africa. Despite having the world's biggest antiretroviral [ARV] treatment programme, South Africa had been paying significantly more than other low and middle-income countries for its antiretroviral drugs. In 2010, bound by the terms of its existing tender for ARVs, the government only bought one third of its products at internationally competitive prices.

Over the following two years, a 53% reduction in the cost of ARVs saved the country $640 million. This new tender introduced three-in-one or fixed-dose combination (FDC) drugs helping to reduce the pill burden and improve adherence to treatment.

South Africa largely funds its HIV and AIDS programmes domestically. However, based on National Strategic Plan 2012-

2016 targets, the gap between funding requirements and available funding for HIV is expected to grow.

The Future of HIV and AIDS in South Africa. South Africa has made great strides in tackling its HIV epidemic in recent years and now has the biggest HIV treatment programme in the world. Moreover, these efforts are now largely funded from South Africa's own resources.

HIV prevention initiatives are having a significant impact on mother-to-child transmission rates in particular, which are falling dramatically. New HIV infections overall have fallen by half in the last decade, however, there are still too many.

While the short term financing of South Africa's HIV epidemic is secure, in the longer term, the government needs to explore other strategies in order to sustain and expand its progress.

All These AIDS "Cures" Are a Fantasy—One That Can Cause Real Harm

Kent Sepkowitz

Kent Sepkowitz is an infectious disease specialist in New York City.

Every chronic disease has around it a cottage industry of treatments, high and low, that prey on the hopes of the often hopeless. Scarcely a week goes by without a new claim about a promising treatment for cancer or Alzheimer's or AIDS being just around the corner, often with the majesty of the word "cure" in the headline. These usually work the high-flying science side of the ledger, with talk of genes being folded or unfolded, DNA being spliced, and new Achilles' heels being revealed, though of course shark cartilage and its descendants are never too far away.

So too are the assertions, once in the backs of magazines or newspapers but now afloat on the Internet, about cures of less threatening but certainly disruptive conditions—hemorrhoids, constipation, heartburn, baldness, low back pain, lower libido. Here the snake oil quotient is a bit more evident than in the skybox seats occupied by insights made using hard science. But the punchline surely is the same: A vitamin, perhaps, or a new salve or a radical change in diet—these simple steps can bring you relief! Today!

Overhyping a Cure

So it is with an extremely cautious eye that I read this week of the latest hopeful AIDS cure, a claim from France that two men, unknown to each other and infected 25 years apart, were cured from HIV infection because of an enzyme that, the scientists suggest, precluded the essential replication of HIV. They found traces of the virus spliced into the person's normal DNA yet could detect no evidence of circulating virus. The two cases were selected from a group of 10 people called "elite controllers," people who without treatment have no detectable virus in their bloodstream or tissue.

It's like finding a new way to boil an egg and claiming you have found the key to stopping global hunger.

Pretty cool stuff, for sure, and possibly credible. The full article, which appears in the journal *Clinical Microbiology and Infection*, the house organ of the venerable European Society of Clinical Microbiology and Infectious Diseases, has as a senior author a giant in the field of infectious diseases, Didier Raoult. He also is the editor of the journal, which seems to publish a lot of interesting if preliminary work.

Their premise is completely plausible. With an infection such as HIV, which affects 35 million people today and has already killed millions and millions, it is certain that odd things occasionally will happen. The one-in-a-million chance is exactly that—a small but real chance, as any lotto winner will tell you.

It is surely no surprise, therefore, that something along the lines of what Raoult and his co-workers describe has taken place; i.e., a person or two has been infected by the virus, but the virus never established a foothold in their body. But the authors and the press once again have shown an overeagerness to invoke the notion that this very early, interesting, possibly correct observation would for sure, or almost for sure, lead to a cure, and maybe really soon. It's like finding a new way to boil an egg and claiming you have found the key to stopping global hunger.

In the rabid claims, the scientists and press have joined a crowded space; there have been other AIDS cure claims. In 2014 alone, we have seen the thrilling "cure" of two babies treated early who in fact were not cured, and the promise of a new approach to treatment, focusing on weak spots in the HIV genome, that would usher in a new day for patients worldwide, and soon-ish.

These investigators, or the swarm following them looking for a read-me headline, seem to have forgotten that not that long ago, HIV was itself in the vitamins-for-baldness, snake oil stage of development. Indeed, in the 1980s many AIDS cures were being touted, including one called MM-1, promoted by an Egyptian rectal surgeon with "unbelievable claims of cure" from his satisfied customers—who only had to fork over $75,000 for the mystery potion. The rumble of headlines this week seems to show that the basic rush-to-judgment itch from the MM-1 days never went really away, it only found classier company.

As I wrote earlier this year, referring to the non-cured "cured" babies, there is real harm in all this blindly and blithely hopeful chatter. Hope, of course, is an essential commodity for anyone facing a substantial illness, and promising developments placed in the not-too-far-off future can become a lifeline for those cornered by a relentless disease. But unsubstantiated hope, hope that rides on the wings of people selling ad space rather than on the shoulders of those making careful scientific observations, represents nothing but a fairy tale. And like a fairy tale, once the fun fantasy has ended, we thud back to the unforgiving and treacherous world of the here and now—which because of the fun distraction feels harsher than ever.

South Africa Is Beating Its AIDS Epidemic

Jina Moore

Jina Moore is a correspondent for the Christian Science Monitor.

When Olga Thimbela first took in the kids, things were rosy. They were young. So was she, for that matter. She had two children of her own, and six more she was determined to raise after their mothers—one a sister and one an aunt of hers—died of AIDS, leaving the children orphaned.

Threat of Decimation

Olga cleaned houses most days, and her husband, Pontsho Monamodi, worked, if irregularly, as a security guard. They brought in enough to support their expanded family, provided they were penny-wise, and they felt buoyed by knowing they were doing the right thing.

That was in 2007, a time that Olga remembers as when "things were easier, when life was simpler." It was also when the [*Christian Science*] *Monitor* first met Olga and her family, who became part of an occasional series on South Africa's AIDS orphans. The disease has killed some 2.3 million people in South Africa, leaving roughly 1 million children without one or both parents. Only 11 percent of those were born with HIV, but all of them face challenges: depression, truancy, sexual vulnerability, and, in some cases, hunger and abuse.

Six years ago, Olga's choice was a bright spot in the bleak story of a continent beset by AIDS. South Africans were living in the worst-hit country in the worst-hit region of the world:

Roughly 22.5 million had HIV, the virus that causes AIDS, in the region in 2007, according to estimates at the time by UN-AIDS, the Joint United Nations Program on HIV/AIDS. That was twice the number of HIV-positive people in every country in the rest of the world combined.

For years, Thabo Mbeki, then South Africa's president, had denied that the disease even existed, and an overburdened health system, social stigma, and political sensitivities made it difficult for many patients to get tested for the disease or to get access to antiretroviral drugs. Experts, meanwhile, were predicting that the population would be decimated—that the men and women who drove the economy with their labor and consumption, who sheltered and raised the nation's children, who financially and emotionally supported their elders and parents, would be wiped out.

After years of outside assistance, more than 80 percent of the [antiretroviral] drugs its people need are paid for by the South African government itself.

"That was not just a kind of ludicrous concern of some activists; that was the real prospect"—and not only in South Africa, according to Christoph Benn, spokesman for The Global Fund to Fight AIDS, Tuberculosis and Malaria, a Geneva-based nonprofit organization.

Infection Has Plummeted

That was nearly a decade ago. Today, Africa's progress in preventing and treating AIDS exceeds even the most optimistic of earlier projections:

- The number of new HIV infections across Africa has dropped by 25 percent since 2001—and more than 50 percent in 13 sub-Saharan African countries—according to the UNAIDS 2012 global report.

- The number of AIDS-related deaths on the continent has fallen by 32 percent since 2005, the worst year for AIDS deaths worldwide.

- Here in South Africa, progress is even sharper. Rates of infection have fallen by at least 30 percent. Nearly 2 million people are on antiretroviral drugs, known as ARVs, which have helped extend the life span of the sick and limit the transmission of the disease. Approximately 75 percent of South Africans who need ARVs have access to them, putting the country just shy of The Global Fund's 80 percent standard for universal access.

- Perhaps most meaningful to ordinary South Africans: Life expectancy in South Africa has gone up—reaching levels not seen since 1995.

According to the US General Accountability Office, the President's Emergency Plan for AIDS Relief [PEPFAR] has spent $1.2 billion providing ARVs since 2003. Between 2008 and 2012, owing to the efforts of PEPFAR, the number of people on ARVs tripled to 5.1 million.

At the end of its second funding cycle, PEPFAR, like other international donors, is focusing on improving national capacity to manage HIV/AIDS. That management includes domestic financing streams, one burden South Africa has taken up. After years of outside assistance, more than 80 percent of the drugs its people need are paid for by the South African government itself. Last year, the South African government announced it would spend $600 million procuring ARVs in 2013 and 2014. Nevertheless, doctors and AIDS activists say supply often falls short of national demand.

But the surprising progress in beating the disease may be bringing about a shift in thinking: AIDS is no longer an acute emergency.

To be sure, it's still a serious epidemic—globally, 34 million people are living with HIV. Eastern Europe and Central Asia, where rates of new infection had been stable for several years, are seeing an increase in new infections, and infection rates in the Middle East and North Africa have increased since 2000, even as every other region in the world saw the numbers go down. And, despite remarkable progress, sub-Saharan Africa is still the region hit hardest by AIDS and accounts for 71 percent of all new infections globally.

Olga's story represents the . . . toll that AIDS has taken, not just on the infected or ill but on South Africa and the hundreds of thousands of caregivers who stepped up to take in these orphans.

Yet increasingly, AIDS is understood as a chronic illness, one that, health experts say, can be managed over a lifetime—a lifetime potentially as long for those living with HIV as those without.

"We can very confidently say that treatment extends the life of [HIV] patients for at least 20 years, maybe more, and [that] many of them can lead perfectly normal lives," says Mr. Benn.

AIDS Takes a Toll on the Uninfected, Too

But that's only half the story. Olga's story represents the other half—the toll that AIDS has taken, not just on the infected or ill but on South Africa and the hundreds of thousands of caregivers who stepped up to take in these orphans.

In 2006, Olga's two cousins joined her four orphaned nephews and a niece at her home, pushing the number of people living in their two-bed, four-room metal shack to 10. Yet Olga and Pontsho were optimistic, and the children seemed happy.

But things changed. By 2010, Olga's older foster children were struggling with school, first loves, and sex. The couple—and their families—were quarreling about the finances and responsibilities associated with caring for so many children. Pontsho moved out, but the couple hoped that the stresses would ease and they could restore their relationship.

That didn't happen.

Pontsho left for good; Olga—who, at age 36 now has 11 biological and foster children—doesn't hear from him anymore. Her older foster children dropped out of school and are having children of their own, children who also ultimately depend on Olga. When members of her extended family hit hard times, or simply when they've had too much to drink, they press her for money; they're convinced a modest state grant for foster parents has made Olga rich. It's far from true. Olga can't work anymore, and her boyfriend's irregular work as a taxi driver brings in a pittance.

It would be a mistake to misunderstand Olga's honesty. She does not seek pity, and she never evinces weakness, not even when she cries.

For years, Olga had been diagnosed with a thyroid problem, which became critical during her last pregnancy. In May [2013], her youngest child was delivered early, and she was taken into emergency surgery to fix the problem. Her doctor says having more children would be life-threatening.

There's an irony, then, in today's story of AIDS in Africa. Just as the world turns a corner, just as so many global public health statistics on AIDS finally get better, and just as patients begin living longer, the people—and they are mostly women—who stepped up in place of the dead are exhausted.

The energy and optimism they harnessed a decade or more ago when they became surrogates to a generation made vulnerable by the loss of its parents have been tried, tested, and worn down.

While the world is learning to manage AIDS, Olga and other women like her experience the disease in a different, nonmedical way. And they represent a cost of the epidemic that hasn't yet factored into most figures.

"Sometimes I think that I'm relieved the kids are growing up. Then come the [grandchildren], then come these," she says, pointing to her two youngest biological children. "I don't know if it's a gift or bad luck. I can't say it's bad luck, because children are a gift from God."

On days when even gifts from God are too much for her, she curls up on her bed and watches the American soap opera "Days of Our Lives." Sometimes that helps. Sometimes it doesn't. And sometimes, she confesses through sobs, "I feel maybe I wish I had never been born."

AIDS Orphan Defies the Odds

It would be a mistake to misunderstand Olga's honesty. She does not seek pity, and she never evinces weakness, not even when she cries. For a woman with few friends and an absentee extended family, speaking with *Monitor* reporters about the challenges of her choices seems to bring a kind of relief. Her openness also reveals her as a person who takes on the weight of the world.

"I have been crying a long time. I been crying inside my heart. . . . I cry when I see myself, the situation that I'm in. Because I try, I try, I try so hard to give my kids a better future, a better life," laments Olga. "But it looks like I fail, you know?

"I keep asking . . . God, maybe I did something wrong, that's why you punish me. Why don't you let the kids alone?" she says.

Yet, her foster daughter Bulelwa Thimbela, who has a 2-year-old daughter, in so many ways has defied the odds. Her mother died of AIDS when Bulelwa was 13, but Bulelwa wasn't born with HIV, and she has Olga, who cares deeply about her. Bulelwa's pregnancy disappointed Olga: The girl was bookish as a youngster, always helping the younger children with their homework. "I thought for sure that one would have a bright future," Olga says.

But studies suggest this isn't unusual for children who lose their parents to AIDS. They are more likely than their peers to drop out of school, to suffer depression, anxiety, and abuse. They are more likely than other children, even other orphans, to be sexually active at an earlier age. They are less likely than other children to use condoms, and girls who have lost their parents to AIDS are more likely to contract HIV, and more likely to trade sex for money or material goods, even when taking factors like poverty into account.

At 16, when Bulelwa became pregnant, she believed she and her baby's father were each other's first sexual partners (though now she suspects he may have been lying about that).

Against this backdrop, Bulelwa is fortunate—and smart. She loved living with Olga, whose home was a place of refuge after being "abused emotionally" by another relative's family. "They used to call us names and shout at us," Bulelwa remembers. "Really I wanted to get out of there."

She felt "free and normal" in Olga's shack in Tshepisong, a township not far from Johannesburg; she devoted herself to school, and she went back as soon as she gave birth. But she dropped out again when she was briefly ill.

At 16, when Bulelwa became pregnant, she believed she and her baby's father were each other's first sexual partners (though now she suspects he may have been lying about that).

Still, they used condoms, like an increasing number of South Africans, but she became pregnant after their birth control failed. Both of them went for HIV tests, which were negative.

The father of Bulelwa's baby is a lecturer at a university some distance from her home, and six months ago, when Bulelwa found out he had a string of other girlfriends, she ended their sexual relationship.

"I told him, 'We must leave this thing, because it's not going anywhere,'" she said. "If he's busy with other girls there, he's going to [get] diseases there and bring them to me."

They remain friends, and he offered to pay tuition for Bulelwa until she can secure the scholarship she lost when she dropped out of school. She'll finish her secondary degree and then specialize in business.

"I want to have my own house, to be an independent woman, and to run a business," she says. "I want to have a big house and a car."

But, she says, she does not want a husband. She lost her mother when she was only 13, and she never knew her father. Most of the adult lives she's seen have disappointed her: "Most of married women, some of them had to give up their dreams so that they could be with their families, and I don't think I will afford that kind of life. I just need to build a bright future for my baby and some of my family."

"Treatment as Prevention"

Around the world, HIV-positive people, too, can dream about raising their children and improving their family's future.

Life expectancies for HIV-positive people may not be that much different than those of people without the disease, says Leigh Johnson, an epidemiologist and actuary at the University of Cape Town and a member of the International Epidemiologic Databases to Evaluate AIDS, a research consortium founded by US government health agencies.

In fact, he says, "I don't even think five years ago we would have expected to see that kind of outcome."

Treatment is doing something else few expected when antiretroviral drugs first appeared in the late 1990s: It's helping prevent the spread of AIDS. If taken regularly, ARVs reduce the presence of the virus to such low levels that an HIV-positive person essentially cannot transmit the virus to a sexual partner.

In Cameroon, Malawi, and Nigeria, . . . the number of men reporting condom usage in their last sexual encounter has gone up in the past 10 years or so.

The UN [United Nations] is pushing for countries to adopt "treatment as prevention" strategies that would widen access to ARVs. The other key prevention measure is condoms. Between 2000 and 2008, HIV incidence dropped by 30 percent, Mr. Johnson and researchers wrote in a 2011 study—and they attributed 37 percent of that drop to condom usage. But access to ARVs has increased since the period reflected in the study. Today, ARVs and condoms, when used "under optimal conditions," are equally effective at preventing the transmission of HIV, says Ade Fakoya, senior adviser for HIV and AIDS at The Global Fund.

Drugs aren't the only prevention strategy, of course. Health workers and donors have been promoting and providing condoms to reduce the transmission of HIV for years; last year, more than one-third of funding went toward promoting "behavioral change"—getting people to have safer sex and fewer partners—and providing condoms. But in some countries, especially in Africa, condoms are still a difficult sell.

"If you use a condom, a man sometimes will feel like he hasn't even had sex," Bulelwa explains.

And UNAIDS data suggests condoms go in and out of fashion. In Cameroon, Malawi, and Nigeria, for example, the number of men reporting condom usage in their last sexual encounter has gone up in the past 10 years or so. But in Uganda, Ivory Coast, and Benin, condom usage is dropping.

Male circumcision is another prevention technique growing in popularity. Researchers say the procedure could prevent as many as 1 in 5 HIV infections, and 13 countries in South and East Africa have begun offering the procedure.

Some countries have also reported wider interventions—to curb infections among "high-risk groups" such as sex workers and men who have sex with men—although the majority of countries don't report any data on these populations at all.

UNAIDS cautions that it's impossible to say which of these interventions has had the greatest impact on reducing new HIV cases; in behavioral change programs, for instance, there are too many factors at work at the same time. There are also the usual caveats about numbers like these in general: Condom usage, for example, is a self-reported number, and researchers know that people frequently lie about their behaviors, often to match an expected norm. And then there's what Johnson calls the "natural dynamics of the epidemic."

"In any epidemic you would expect to see some kind of saturation effect, where people who are most at risk of infection get infected early on in the epidemic, and then you start to see incidence rates decline," he says.

ARVs: A New Lifestyle

Over time, ARVs have become cheaper and easier to distribute. "You can now deliver those drugs in pretty simple health centers in rural areas," Benn, of The Global Fund, says. That allows health workers to "reach populations at a level we had not imagined would be possible before."

Development of generic drugs has made a major contribution to the affordability of ARVs. So, too, has the purchasing power of donors like The Global Fund and PEPFAR. Benn says that The Global Fund can buy a year's supply of ARVs for one patient for $100. (With transport, management, and administrative costs, the price of an annual supply is closer to $400.)

South African politics has changed dramatically in the past 10 years, and today the nation itself finances 82 percent of the ARVs provided to South Africans, according to Benn. That's a big change: In 2001, the government was still denying that HIV caused AIDS, and the only organization offering South Africans ARVs was Doctors Without Borders (known by its French acronym, MSF).

So if there's an emblem of this dramatic change, it's Khayelitsha, a massive township on the edge of Cape Town. Here, in 2007, MSF piloted ARV "adherence clubs," a group of no more than 30 stable HIV-positive patients who meet every two months to get weighed, pick up their medication, and discuss treatment or life challenges.

The clubs are run by laypeople—not doctors or nurses—who coordinate with pharmacists on drug delivery and keep relevant basic medical records. If patients stay stable, they only have to meet a nurse or doctor once a year, for a full checkup.

> *If there's an emblem of this dramatic change, it's Khayelitsha, a massive township on the edge of Cape Town.*

Xolelwa Xabendlini appreciates this efficiency. She works every day as a housekeeper, pulling in about $300 a month for the seven people in her household, for which she is the only breadwinner.

"We don't have to wait in this queue you see outside," she says, gesturing toward the door beyond which more than 100 people sit and wait to see a nurse and receive their ARVs. That means that Ms. Xabendlini knows she can get to her job on time, and she won't have to choose between earning a day's wage and picking up her medicine.

Other clubs meet in private homes, church halls, or public libraries. All that convenience seems to be paying off. A study published earlier this year found that 97 percent of patients in MSF's adherence clubs stayed with their treatment regimens, compared with 85 percent of those seen only in clinics. MSF's 20 adherence clubs have grown, over the past six years, to more than 600 in the Cape Town region, reaching as many as 18,000 people in a wider rollout by the provincial government.

If the idea of simplifying access and meeting patients near their homes seems almost obvious today, years ago it was revolutionary. The stigma surrounding AIDS was so corrosive that picking up AIDS drugs in the neighborhood, and thus risking recognition and public exposure, would have been unthinkable for most patients. So, too, was the idea of taking treatment out of the hands of specialists at hospitals.

Today, though, Xabendlini says, people are—and must be—more open. She talks freely with neighbors about the trips she makes to pick up her ARVs, which she's cheerfully nicknamed "chappies," after a local brand of bubble gum.

"In my street, lots of people died with HIV," she says. "If I tell them I'm also HIV positive, they think I'm lying. They see I'm strong and always laughing. I can't take this [into] my head because it would make me crazy."

Elizabeth Molomo echoes Xabendlini's optimism, and has a bit more experience behind it: She has been living with HIV for 15 years. She lives in Soweto, the largest township in Johannesburg. Every morning at 6:45, her cellphone alarm goes off, reminding her to take her ARVs. Her eldest daughter calls, too.

"I don't see myself as a sick person," she says. "I take myself as a healed person."

Australia's AIDS Crisis Is Over

Abigail Groves

Abigail Groves is a freelance writer and a former policy analyst at the Australian Federation of AIDS Organizations.

Films like *Dallas Buyers Club*, which won Matthew McConaughey an Oscar®, and *United in Anger*, a history of ACT UP [AIDS activist agency], have turned HIV activists into heroes.

But what is striking about these movies is that the events they depict are placed firmly in an historical context. This is a time that has passed.

A Past Crisis

The urgency of the AIDS crisis has largely, and thankfully, disappeared—at least in the developed west. Yet there is a certain nostalgia for the innovation and excitement that AIDS activism generated.

'People are suddenly interested in talking to me,' says Lloyd Grosse, Sydney [Australia] DJ and former HIV activist. 'It's like we are the heroes of the AIDS movement.'

Grosse lays claim to being the first Australian to come out publicly as HIV-positive and an old, yellowed copy of the *Sydney Star Observer* suggests he may be right. It carries a picture of Grosse in an ad encouraging gay men to 'take control' and get tested for HIV.

The piece now seems innocuous—another ad for HIV services, of the kind familiar to any reader of the gay press. More striking to me are the bouffant hairstyles and high-waisted pants of the early '90s. But there is something from the *Syd-*

ney Star Observer of twenty years ago that I had forgotten: the awful, gut-wrenching death notices.

'There was one period,' Lloyd says, 'when the Bobby Goldsmith Foundation had five clients and seven friends die in one week. One week.' Events like these put Lloyd Grosse's decision to come out in perspective.

There was a real fear, at that time, that the government would put us in quarantine or something like that.

'An activist,' writes Eve Ensler, author of *The Vagina Monologues*, 'is someone who cannot help but fight for something. That person is not usually motivated by a need for power, or money, or fame, but in fact driven slightly mad by some injustice, some cruelty, some unfairness. So much so that he or she is driven by some internal moral engine to act to make it better.'

'They were terrible times, just terrible. I was angry,' says Paul Kidd, a former president of Living Positive Victoria and self-identified "stirrer." Anger, Paul feels, was an appropriate response.

'Anger is what gets people off their arses in the first place, so it has a motivating role. Second, the expression of anger is an important part of activism. There's a time to be respectful and polite, and there's a time to be loud and furious.' Being a gay man in the 1980s and early 90s was one such time.

'At one stage,' Lloyd Grosse recalls, 'ACON [AIDS Council of New South Wales] was telling people not to get tested, because there was nothing that they could do to help us. And there was a real fear, at that time, that the government would put us in quarantine or something like that.'

Acting Up

Grosse later did get tested and, despite assurances that he was not high risk, tested positive. With a background in the union movement, activism came naturally to him.

Already a volunteer at AIDS organisations in Sydney, he became involved with PLWHA (NSW) (today known as Positive Life NSW) and then ACT UP.

Similarly Paul Kidd, who was diagnosed in the early 1990s, says that, 'I've always been a politically aware/outspoken person and AIDS was the issue du jour in the gay community. I thought I was going to die and I wanted to make some noise before I did.'

Not everyone had such a background, though. Lyle Chan is a classical composer who found himself in the middle of an emergency.

'I couldn't stand by,' says Chan. 'My friends were dying. I saw ordinary people turn themselves into activists, so I did the same. The prevailing atmosphere was, "we will do whatever it takes." I was a musician, but I also had a background in molecular biology—though no one was an expert in AIDS back then,' he adds.

'The doctors and researchers had an advantage because of their medical training but still, they knew no more about AIDS than the activists did, because we made a point of being well-informed.' After coming to Australia from America, he joined ACT UP and also ran a 'buyers' club' at ACON, importing drugs from the US unavailable in Australia. Chan had over 400 clients.

The process for approving new drugs was very bureaucratic and took no account of the nature of the illness.

'The AIDS Council gave it a euphemistic name: the Treatments Access Scheme. The buyers club operated under cover of a provision in federal law that allowed people to import certain medical drugs under certain conditions.

'The law was designed for drugs manufactured by legitimate drug companies—but I was importing ddC [dideoxycytidine—an early antiretroviral medication] made in underground laboratories in violation of multiple drug patents, while the official drug company and the Australian government took their time working out how to supply it.'

Access to Treatment

Access to treatments was the big issue for people with HIV in Australia, as it was elsewhere. Access to treatments gave ACT UP its moment in Australia. In Australia, the early trials of AZT—the first antiretroviral drug approved for use by the US Food and Drug Administration—were run on a quota system.

This meant that those who were unable to access the trial were left with nothing, which incensed activists. 'The process for approving new drugs was very bureaucratic and took no account of the nature of the illness. You could have a drug for dandruff and a drug for cancer and they were both treated in exactly the same way,' explains Lyle.

Treatment issues also gave the impetus to ACT UP, the direct action group which had proved effective in the US. However, ACT UP was never as popular or widespread in Australia as it was in the US.

This may have been due to the effectiveness of the Australian government's response to HIV. With a Labor government in power during the 1980s, Australia benefitted from progressive leadership on HIV issues.

'It was really down to three people,' says Lloyd Grosse.

'Neal Blewett was the Health Minister. Bill Whittaker was a great advocate. And Bill Bowtell who was Blewett's advisor—he was in the right place at the right time.'

It was through their leadership that Australia adopted harm minimisation policies such as needle exchanges, and funded organisations like the AIDS Councils to provide community-based education and services. But these community-based services could themselves become targets of attack from activists.

'A lot of my anger was directed at the AIDS movement,' says Lloyd Grosse. 'They were too caught up with their careers—they would never stick their necks out.'

Lyle Chan says ACT UP deliberately cultivated its image as the 'lunatic fringe' of the HIV movement.

'ACT UP had a love-hate relationship with organisations like ACON,' he recalls.

'ACT UP criticised the HIV organisations and could also say and do things that other groups couldn't. But we also knew that our extreme protests against government officials and drug companies would send them straight into negotiations with ACON (the AIDS Council of NSW) and AFAO (the Australian Federation of AIDS Organisations) to get relief.'

Once it became clear, between 1994 and 1996, that we were no longer fighting against a constant backdrop of death, it became possible to imagine a future where every day was not a state of emergency.

These organisations had the same goals as ACT UP but were less antagonistic. The range of players—government, medical professionals, drug companies, NGOs [nongovernmental organizations] and activist groups—made for a volatile environment, especially when sex and personal relationships were added into the mix.

Leaving Activism

Where has it gone, this anger? Lyle Chan says he made a conscious decision to leave activism behind, once it became clear that the protease inhibitors, the new generation of antiretroviral drugs, would 'rescue people from the toilet.'

'Activism is an attempt to reach some kind of normality,' he reflects, 'that you feel is being denied for some reason. Once it became clear, between 1994 and 1996, that we were no longer fighting against a constant backdrop of death, it became possible to imagine a future where every day was not a state of emergency.

'Some activists continued, working in Asia for instance, where the crisis continued for different social reasons. But I felt my work as an activist was done, and with normality came the responsibility of returning to my true purpose, which was to write music.'

Chan has since written an acclaimed string quartet memoir of his years as an AIDS activist.

Lloyd Grosse is no longer involved in HIV issues, either, though he says he took longer to move on.

'The war ended,' he says. 'People are no longer dying, so in a sense we won. I have returned to my core, which is social justice issues.'

Paul Kidd, who became involved in AIDS activism a little later than the others, says he is no longer angry—at least, not about HIV issues.

'Anger doesn't seem right in the current context because the stakes just aren't as high as they once were: people are not dying.' Kidd, however, still writes about HIV issues.

'I think our AIDS organisations have become dreadfully risk-averse,' he says. 'Too many of them are more concerned about upsetting their funders than doing what is right to protect people's rights and lives. I think it's important to have independent voices calling out and questioning the AIDS establishment and I try to continue doing that in my way.'

Australia and the Rest of the World

All readily acknowledged that while the AIDS crisis is over in Australia, it is still very present in other parts of the world. The International AIDS Conference in Melbourne [July 2014] will see some of the world's most inspiring AIDS activists in Australia.

Paul Kidd is hopeful that the conference will re-invigorate Australian activists. 'I think the AIDS conference will be an energising force for HIV activism in Australia,' he says.

'I hope it will generate some anger and some willingness to challenge the status quo. It will also help local people see where they fit in the global picture, and maybe contextualise the local challenges and local complacencies in terms of a broader picture.'

Researchers Have Renewed Hope for an HIV Cure

Mary Engel

Mary Engel is a staff writer at the Fred Hutchinson Cancer Research Center in Seattle, Washington.

Until about five years ago, cure was the forbidden word of the HIV world: No one said it out loud.

From Impossible to Possible

In the awful early years of the pandemic, researchers struggled to find treatments to stem the tide of deaths. To suggest a cure was possible, much less imminent, seemed not just naive but cruel.

A cure remained elusive even after combination antiretroviral therapy in the mid-1990s turned HIV from an automatic death sentence to a manageable chronic disease. For those with access to it, the treatment was a life-saving breakthrough, yes, but no more a cure than insulin is a cure for diabetes. Scientists learned that reservoirs of latent HIV-infected cells hide in the body, out of reach of the drugs. Stop taking a daily pill, and the virus comes roaring back.

But today, scientists are not just using the word cure, they're organizing whole conferences around it. A cure symposium has been added to the International AIDS Society conference on treatment and prevention, to be held in July in Melbourne, Australia. Fresh from that meeting, society president and Nobel laureate Francoise Barre-Sinoussi—who in 1983 co-discovered the virus that causes AIDS—will speak in August at Fred Hutchinson Cancer Research Center's second Conference on Cell and Gene Therapy for HIV Cure.

To be clear, caution still prevails. Many, including Barre-Sinoussi, say that the most realistic goal may be a so-called "functional cure" that doesn't necessarily eradicate all traces of the virus but eliminates the need to take daily pills. Scientists are also careful not to raise hopes that a cure of any kind will be widely available any time soon.

What can we expect in the next five years?

"If you're talking about a handful or a roomful of people who have been cured of HIV—that's something we're likely to see," said Dr. Keith Jerome, an expert in viral infections at the Hutch's Vaccine and Infectious Diseases and co-host of the upcoming Hutch conference. "If you're talking about something that's broadly available to hundreds of thousands or millions of people, we're much farther away from that."

[Timothy Ray Brown] has not taken antiretroviral medicine since the first transplant and his virus has not rebounded, giving him the distinction of being the first person pronounced—however cautiously—cured of HIV.

Jerome and Dr. Hans-Peter Kiem, a stem cell transplant researcher in the Hutch's Clinical Research Division and conference co-host, lead a team that is investigating using genetically modified stem cells to cure HIV. Their approach is based on the case that first prompted scientists to dare say cure out loud when it was reported in 2008—that of Timothy Ray Brown.

The Game Changer

Seattle-born Brown, now 48, was the keynote speaker last year at the Hutch's first HIV conference. Known in early reports as the Berlin patient, he was diagnosed with HIV in 1995 in Germany, where he was then living, and used antiretroviral therapy to control it. Then he developed acute myeloid leukemia and in 2007, needed a stem cell transplant, a procedure pioneered at the Hutch.

His German doctor decided to try to cure not just the cancer but HIV by finding a stem cell donor who carried two copies of an exceedingly rare gene mutation that confers natural resistance to the virus. The mutation deletes what is known as the delta-32 section of the CCR5 gene, which HIV latches onto and uses to enter white blood cells.

Brown's leukemia returned after the first transplant, so he had a second in 2008 and has remained cancer-free. He has not taken antiretroviral medicine since the first transplant and his virus has not rebounded, giving him the distinction of being the first person pronounced—however cautiously—cured of HIV.

In 2013, scientists published a report of a second cure that occurred through different means: An HIV-infected newborn known as the Mississippi baby was treated immediately after birth with aggressive antiretroviral therapy. The child, now 3, went off treatment after 18 months and didn't have any detectable levels of HIV, but in 2014, evidence of the virus returned. In March of 2014, researchers announced similar results with a second baby who had been born positive, but she is still on the antiretroviral drugs so it's too early to know if she's in remission. Efforts are underway to replicate the results in other newborns.

Timothy Brown's cure launched the cure effort in the United States.

As for the Brown cure, defeatHIV, as Jerome and Kiem's group is called, is not trying to re-create it exactly. A stem cell transplant using donor cells is a last-resort treatment requiring a complex match between donor and recipient as well as a brutal regimen of chemotherapy to kill off the old immune system. Both expensive and risky, such treatment would not be considered appropriate for the vast majority of people with HIV unless they faced a similar life-threatening cancer. Even then, finding a matching donor with two copies of the rare mutation would add to the challenge.

Instead, defeatHIV will use Brown's case as a blueprint for attempting a new kind of therapy involving gene modification. The plan is to take an HIV-infected patient's own stem cells and knock out or disable the gene that acts as the HIV doorway, mimicking the genetics of someone who has natural resistance. The modified cells would then be returned to the patient.

Reports of Brown's cure came at a time when Kiem's lab already had been working on improving techniques to modify and correct hematopoietic stem cells—the precursors that generate all the specialized cells of the blood and immune systems—to treat patients with cancer, genetic blood disorders and chronic infections. The new line of research is designed to answer the question: Can gene therapies generate enough HIV-resistant cells to lead to a cure?

The Collaborators

DefeatHIV started in 2011 with a $20 million grant from the National Institutes of Health [NIH] intended to foster public-private partnerships in working toward an HIV cure. Other members of the team include researchers from the University of Washington, Seattle Children's, The City of Hope's Beckman Research Institute in Duarte, California, and Sangamo BioSciences in Richmond, California.

"Timothy Brown's cure launched the cure effort in the United States," said Kiem. "It's quite remarkable to think that one person has had such an influence on research direction and on the NIH."

The Hutch-led collaboration is one of three distinct approaches funded by the NIH and called the Martin Delaney collaboratories, after an early HIV/AIDS educator and activist. The University of North Carolina, Chapel Hill, is leading a team working on an approach called "shock and kill" or "kick and kill" that is looking for drugs that can wake the virus from its latency stage so that antiretroviral drugs can kill the hidden reservoirs. A group based at the University of California, San Francisco is focused on the role of the immune system and the inflammatory reaction to establishing and maintaining the reservoir.

According to Jerome and Kiem, a successful cure will likely borrow from all three. Drugs used to wake up the viruses could facilitate gene therapy approaches by making them work more efficiently, they said. Inflammation plays a big part not only in HIV persistence but in engraftment of genetically engineered cells.

"We collaborate among the collaboratories," Jerome said. "The ultimate cure is very likely to be a combination of approaches."

Does a Cure Still Matter?

Neither Jerome nor Kiem are worried at the moment about whether these efforts might lead to a so-called "sterilizing cure" that actually wipes out the virus or a functional cure. Working in a cancer research center, they have a keen appreciation of interim steps. In any case, the answer to that is years away, after the therapy is developed, and ways are found to reliably measure the reservoir and clinical trials follow patients over numerous years.

"From the leukemia or lymphoma malignancy point of view, if we don't detect any disease after about 5 years, we talk about cure," said Kiem. "But sometimes the disease comes back even after five or six or seven years. As with cancer, long-term monitoring of patients who might be cured of HIV will be critical."

Does a cure still matter, given what antiretroviral drugs have already accomplished?

To Jerome, Kiem and other scientists, the answer is an urgent yes. Lifelong treatment—although far better than the alternative—is expensive. Not everyone can tolerate the side effects. And despite great progress in recent years in making treatment available, only about 10 million of the 35 million people infected with HIV worldwide are on antiretroviral medication.

Another reason to press for a cure is the risk that the rapidly mutating virus will develop strains that are resistant to the drugs now used to suppress it.

"The general public in the United States doesn't see HIV as an especially urgent problem now because they don't see people visibly dying from the virus," said Jerome. "But if we look at the problem from a worldwide basis, it absolutely is urgent. There's a huge worldwide burden of disease and death from this virus. So, yes, we're going absolutely as fast as we can."

CHAPTER 4

What Are Other Controversies About Deadly Viruses?

Chapter Preface

The human papillomavirus (HPV) is the most common sexually transmitted infection in the world; almost 80 percent of people acquire it at some point in their lives. While in most instances the virus disappears on its own, in some cases HPV can lead to more serious health issues, such as cervical cancer. An HPV vaccine was developed in 2006, and many public health officials now recommend vaccination of preteen girls. This recommendation, however, has proved controversial.

Proponents of the vaccine argue that it may be able to reduce deaths from cervical cancer by two-thirds. A study published by the Centers for Disease Control and Prevention in 2013 showed that high-risk strains of the virus were reduced by half between 2006 and 2010, after the vaccine was introduced. This occurred despite the fact that only a third of teenaged girls in the United States received the full three doses of the vaccine. Other countries, such as Rwanda, have attained vaccination rates of 80 percent and higher. It is thought that increasing the vaccination rate could prevent 53,000 cases of cervical cancer and 17,000 deaths—figures that prompted *The New York Times* to strongly recommend that doctors and parents vaccinate young girls.

There remains significant resistance to the HPV vaccine, however. Some opposition comes from those opposed to any mandatory vaccines—the so-called anti-vaxxers. US senator Michelle Bachmann, for example, claimed falsely that the vaccine could cause mental retardation. Some oppose the vaccine because they feel that young children should not be vaccinated for sexually transmitted diseases since the children are not yet sexually active. There was also resentment of a Texas program, in which all girls entering sixth grade had to be vaccinated unless they were granted a religious or philosophical exemption.

Charlotte Haug, writing for the *New Scientist*, rejects Bachmann's false claims about health dangers but does argue that the vaccine is relatively new, and that its effectiveness is uncertain. For example, she says that vaccine proponents tend to assume that the vaccine offers lifelong protection, which it may not. Long-term side-effects to the vaccine are also unknown at this time. "With so many essential questions unanswered," Huag concludes, "there is good reason to be cautious about introducing large-scale HPV vaccination."[1]

The rest of this chapter looks at other controversies involving deadly viruses, including smallpox, polio, and influenza.

---

1. Charlotte Haug, "We Need to Talk About HPV Vaccination—Seriously," *New Scientist*, September 16, 2011. http://www.newscientist.com/article/dn20928-we-need-to-talk -about-hpv-vaccination--seriously.html#.VTaPlGahDS8.

Save the Smallpox Virus

David Boze

David Boze is a talk radio host on AM 770 KTTH in Seattle and the author of The Little Red Book of Obamunism.

Many people seek to save the whales, save the wolves, save the cuddly polar bears that look simply adorable from a distance of a half-continent away (where they cannot reach your throat), and some even seek to save California's Delta Smelt [a fish] which seem almost worthless until you stop and consider how much farmland they can turn into desert. In justifying protection measures for these creatures, politicians appeal to our desire to pass the splendor and diversity of Creation on to future generations while scientists cite the value of every species for future research—every species, that is, but one.

Not Cute, but Worth Saving

Perhaps it's because it lacks the white fur of the polar bear, the noble eyes of the wolf, or even the pathetic helplessness of the Delta Smelt, but somehow the smallpox virus has yet to enjoy protected status. True, even the razor claws and teeth of a polar bear look cute on a cub, while the offspring of smallpox tend to be painful, puss-filled, scarring hives and hideous death, none of which would sell well on a poster. But since when did adorable offspring become a necessary prerequisite for protection? Though it has yet to set a timeline, just days ago the World Health Organization reaffirmed its commitment to eliminating this tiny little creature from its last *known* habitats, the Atlanta Centers for Disease Control in the United States, and the State Research Center of Virology and Biotechnology in Russia.

I know what you're thinking: After seeing the Russian obsession with security and containment at Chernobyl, [following a nuclear reactor failure in 1986] perhaps little smallpox survives elsewhere too, but alas, it doesn't—that we know of. Unofficially, it might. After all, defectors from the old Evil Empire [the Soviet Union] told tales of vastly larger habitats made for Soviet and perhaps Soviet Satellite countries' weapons programs, but until these virus stores are found accidentally or on purpose, we have to assume only two habitats remain. And assuming is about the best we can do, because apparently when smallpox stores were eradicated and confined to their last two remaining habitats, no inspections were carried out to ensure other nations had destroyed their samples. Of course, when you're dealing with this kind of deadly virus with bio-weapon potential, it's best to trust and not verify. You'll sleep better just not knowing.

We are not as sure as officialdom would have us believe that the smallpox virus has been permanently eliminated.

Our endangered little friend could show up as a surprise somewhere. Recently, the *Wall Street Journal* ran a story about a "bizarre bits" museum exhibit in Virginia that displayed a note from 1873. On this note was pinned the scab of a smallpox victim. Apparently, museum officials decided the odds were minimal that anything catchy was left on it, but somehow, minimal odds weren't enough to convince spoiled sports at the CDC [Centers for Disease Control and Prevention] who arrived in biohazard suits to collect the sample and confine it to a secured facility.

Nothing found on the scab was contagious, or at least that's the official story the public was given to make us feel better. It worked. I know I felt better. Nothing happened and crisis was averted. The last stocks of smallpox are still alone . . . or are they?

We Can't Be Sure Smallpox Is Gone

The story in the *WSJ* and the precautions taken in that incident suggest that we are not as sure as officialdom would have us believe that the smallpox virus has been permanently eliminated. We're pretty sure, but definitely not "I'd bet my life there's no way to catch smallpox" sure. And don't you want to be *that* sure when it comes to this subject? Let's face it, it's okay to be sure about the capital of Iowa and end up being wrong, but it's not OK to be sure that a scab attached to a letter isn't carrying a disease that will wipe out a third of the human population and turn out to be wrong. OK, maybe I'm exaggerating about the third, but if you're among the first exposed, I think you'd appreciate the hyperbole. Museum officials suggested that countless artifacts are out there similar to their scab-on-letter display. What if one of those future items ends up with a big surprise?

Reportedly, scientists who study the virus want it preserved for further research and vaccine development and generally scientists who do not specifically study the virus seem more anxious for its elimination. In a Sky News story, an advocate for eliminating remaining smallpox samples said, "There is no good scientific reason for keeping them, we already know all we need to know about the smallpox virus." This struck me as an odd thing for a professor to say. How could we know *all* we need to know or be sure we can even predict *all* we might ever need to know? How could we be sure that further study of the virus would not yield additional important information? Is it not possible that in the future new methods of inquiry might reveal information not yet imagined?

Let's review: A 135-year-old letter prompted officials to take precautions in case of deadly contagion, and countless additional relics of this kind are thought spread throughout the world. The former Soviet Stock is likely a whole lot bigger than the Russians are saying, but officially it's not. At least some scientists who specifically study the virus want stocks preserved for further study. And the good guys (that's us) can safely contain, study and use this stock with the potential to create advances in vaccines.

In the face of this threat, it's time little smallpox was added to the endangered species list.

Yet, smallpox is still threatened with extinction. WHO [World Health Organization] has delayed setting the date of destruction, but remains determined on a course of elimination.

Retain For Study

As long as there's a chance of Variola smallpox virus showing up to plague mankind again—or even something similar to it, and having possession of samples of the smallpox virus may give us an advantage in waging war against it, does it not seem prudent to maintain the samples and switch the debate from destruction of these final stocks to redundancies in the safeguards of their preservation?

In the face of this threat, it's time little smallpox was added to the endangered species list. After all, a potential species only has to hit one of five criteria and smallpox snags at least three: There is threatened destruction of its habitat; it's declining due to predation (we've killed about all of it); and there are manmade factors that could affect its continued existence. Heck three out five should be a slam dunk.

One thing, though: let's skip re-introducing this one into the wild.

Eliminate the Smallpox Virus

Gareth Williams

Gareth Williams is emeritus professor of medicine at the University of Bristol, United Kingdom, and author of Angel of Death: The Story of Smallpox.

Delegates from across the world will meet next week [May 2014] at the World Health Organization [WHO] in Geneva, Switzerland, to consider an irrevocable act: the deliberate and final extinction of a species.

Not Quite Extinct

Everyone agrees that the world is a better place without this particular species roaming free. There was universal celebration when it was all but wiped out more than three decades ago. Even so, the WHO debate stands a fair chance of stalling because the group is well practised in not quite making things happen where this species is concerned. It will be the sixth attempt to resolve this issue. So what's going on?

The species is the *Variola* virus, which causes smallpox, and the group deciding its fate will be the 67th World Health Assembly, the WHO's decision-making body.

At its height, smallpox killed 1 person in 12 and mutilated hundreds of millions more. During the 20th century, vaccination steadily edged it towards extinction. Like most doctors of my generation, I never saw a case after qualifying in 1977 and hopefully never will, because the global eradication of smallpox was confirmed in 1980.

The disease may have disappeared globally but the virus is not extinct. After eradication, the WHO closed smallpox research labs across the world and destroyed all stocks of the virus except for two duplicate sets of representative strains, which were kept for research in two high-security establishments. This was in 1983, when US president Ronald Reagan's Star Wars initiative dominated the headlines. In true cold war symmetry, the WHO handed one batch to the US Centers for Disease Control (CDC) in Atlanta, Georgia, and the other to the State Research Centre for Virology and Biotechnology in Koltsovo, Novosibirsk, then part of Soviet Russia. At both sites, the virus samples were locked away in liquid nitrogen. The WHO has repeatedly postponed the date of destruction because of US and Russian opposition.

Not much has changed since the last time the stockpiles were spared in 2011. Experimental smallpox drugs are in the pipeline. The intact virus is pretty redundant as a research tool: the genomes of many strains have been thoroughly sequenced and key proteins required by the functioning virus can be made in the lab. Over the last 30 years, the stocks of virus have contributed little to scientific understanding, other than confirming that new drugs aimed at other viruses still plaguing us are not much use against smallpox.

The Variola *virus is a genie which must not be allowed to escape from its bottle into the world again.*

Removing Risk

The Advisory Group of Independent Experts, convened by the WHO, recently argued that keeping the virus will never serve any useful purpose. It has been overruled by another expert committee, also convened by the WHO; the Advisory Committee on Variola Virus Research says the stockpile can help the work on antiviral treatments.

Talk of the need for new treatments is undoubtedly influenced by past misuse of the virus for military ends and contemporary fears that terrorists or a rogue state might commandeer smallpox as a bioweapon.

During the 1760s, the English hatched a plot to exterminate Native Americans by deliberately infecting them via blankets that had been exposed to smallpox. They didn't wipe them out, but many died. This theme was picked up and refined 200 years later by the Russians. It is an unfortunate coincidence that their highly virulent strains of weapons-grade smallpox were developed at the VECTOR germ warfare laboratory in Koltsovo, on the same site that now houses the virus stock that was entrusted to the Soviet Union.

The *Variola* virus is a genie which must not be allowed to escape from its bottle into the world again. The chances of smallpox being released, inadvertently or deliberately, from either the CDC site or Koltsovo are vanishingly small, given the elaborate security.

However, that risk will never be zero while stocks remain. Destruction removes that risk and might allow the WHO to focus on what we will really need if smallpox ever comes back, either because a related virus evolves to replace it, or a human villain releases some unknown cache.

There is no proven treatment for smallpox and our vaccines, while effective, are in short supply. The vaccine issue is where we should focus our efforts. A handful of countries have enough to immunise just 20 per cent of their populations; the WHO used to hold hundreds of millions of doses but destroyed most when freezer space was in short supply during the 1990s. In an emergency, it would take months for vaccine production to get up to speed, and even then this would be on a pathetically small scale.

Today's transport networks are capable of spreading the virus quickly through the biggest susceptible population in the history of our species. Immunity was lost as vaccination, which carries health risks, stopped soon after eradication. So a smallpox outbreak could easily become a global catastrophe, which the WHO's stocks of *Variola* would do nothing to mitigate.

So what should happen in Geneva next week? Above all, the World Health Assembly should vote to destroy the stocks of *Variola* virus without further delay. This would prevent yet another unedifying and expensive cycle of indecision. If the threat of smallpox staging a comeback is at all credible then our capacity to deal with it must also be credible.

Also, we must not forget the wider significance of smallpox. It is not just one of the nastier exhibits in the museum of medical horrors. It is the only human infection that we have successfully exterminated. It is time for the WHO to move on.

Do Not Require Flu Vaccines for Health-care Workers

Michael Gardam, Camille Lemieux, and Susy Hota

Michael Gardam, Camille Lemieux, and Susy Hota are medical doctors with the infection prevention and control unit of the Toronto University Health Network.

There has been a good deal of recent media attention regarding what some see as a medical and ethical imperative that health-care workers be vaccinated against influenza. This view stems from two conclusions: vaccinating health-care workers protects patients from influenza-related harm, and current strategies have not been successful in achieving high vaccination rates.

Vaccine Does Not Ensure Protection

Some Canadian jurisdictions want to see vaccination made mandatory while others want to mandate that unvaccinated workers wear a mask while at work throughout the influenza season.

Unfortunately, this issue is not as black and white as it has been portrayed: the evidence supporting influenza vaccination is not definitive and a lack of evidence and practical concerns make mandated masking a dubious policy.

More than 200 viruses can cause "influenza-like illness" and influenza is typically responsible for only 10 to 15 per cent of such illness each season. The majority of people who say they have "the flu" will not have influenza. Influenza vaccination does not protect against illness due to these other vi-

Michael Gardam, Camille Lemieux, and Susy Hota, "The Case Against Mandatory Flu Vaccination for Health Care Workers," *Commentary*, July 28, 2014. Copyright © 2014 Michael Gardam. All rights reserved. Reproduced with permission.

ruses. Some of these, such as respiratory syncytial virus, are being increasingly recognized as a dangerous pathogen affecting the elderly.

The debated evidence supporting vaccinating workers in long-term care has been used as justification to aggressively expand vaccination of workers to all health-care settings.

How well does the influenza vaccine work? On average, it is about 60-per-cent effective in protecting against influenza, although in some years, it is far less effective. Protection wanes as the influenza season wears on and by springtime its protective effect can be negligible. Some years the Centers for Disease Control and Prevention have recommended the use of prophylactic medications during outbreaks in vaccinated people because we cannot trust that the vaccine properly protects them. A renowned research group concluded last year that the public health community has been guilty of overestimating vaccine effectiveness in order to encourage vaccination.

The evidence supporting vaccinating health care workers to protect patients is controversial. A recent meta-analysis that included the best studies showed that health-care worker vaccination does not protect patients from getting or dying from influenza but rather decreases deaths from any cause, and reduced influenza-like illness. The authors concluded that the best explanation for these confusing results was that the studies were biased. Unfortunately when conclusions such as these are published, they are often discounted when they should at least make us pause and think. Another recent meta-analysis found that vaccination had minimal impact on employee absenteeism.

Debated Evidence

Surprisingly, the debated evidence supporting vaccinating workers in long-term care has been used as justification to aggressively expand vaccination of workers to all health-care settings, including clinics where a patient might only spend a few minutes with a health-care worker.

So what about making unvaccinated health-care workers wear a mask at all times while at work? It is not clear how well wearing a mask while healthy would prevent infection, as this has never been studied as a strategy to prevent influenza. Studies have shown that a mask continually can at best cause discomfort, and at worst hinder patient care by impeding communication and increasing provider errors. It could easily be seen to be a punitive measure. Given the limitations of the vaccine and the other causes of influenza-like illness, an enforced approach requiring workers to wear a mask if coming to work ill (whether or not they have been vaccinated) or better yet, just staying home, makes more intuitive sense.

People who decline influenza vaccination state a wide range of reasons, many of which we neither understand nor agree with; however these beliefs are a reality that public health has to deal with. If public health leaders downplay vaccine limitations while at the same time engaging in heavy-handed strategies to drive vaccination, they will only be emboldening anti-vaccinationist beliefs by providing more evidence that the medical establishment is untrustworthy.

A savvy public armed with ever-greater levels of medical knowledge is growing frustrated with the absolute pronouncements of modern medicine and will likely challenge them. What will more half-truths bring for the future?

We get the influenza vaccine every year and encourage others to do so. Despite its shortcomings, it is the only vaccine we have right now; however, we stop short at forcing individuals to be vaccinated against influenza, either through mandatory programs or pseudo-mandatory programs such as "vaccine or mask." This grey issue has too many caveats to justify taking away an individual's autonomy.

There are serious patient safety issues in our hospitals. It is time to stop focusing on heavy-handed policies based on questionable evidence and move forward to strategies that engage health-care workers in making patient safety a top priority.

Bird Flu Research Will Not Create a Bioweapon

Peter Christian Hall

Peter Christian Hall is the author of the novel American Fever: A Tale of Romance & Pestilence.

Amid the furor over the U.S. government's move to restrict publication of vital research into H5N1 avian flu, no one seems to be challenging a key assumption—that H5N1 could make a useful weapon. It wouldn't.

Research Should Be Free

The National Science Advisory Board for Biosecurity recently pressured *Science* and *Nature* not to fully publish two widely discussed papers detailing separate efforts to devise an H5N1 avian flu strain that transmits easily in ferrets and might do so among human beings. The proposed solution is to issue redacted versions and circulate details only to approved institutions.

This unprecedented interference in the field of biology could hinder research and hamper responsiveness in distant lands plagued by H5N1. If institutions there don't know what gene changes to watch for, how quickly will we know if H5N1 replicates a pandemic combination defined by researchers on three continents?

There's little question that this fearsome virus could wreak catastrophic harm if it learns how to circulate readily among humans. Through last week [January 2012], when H5N1 killed a man near Hong Kong (site of the first official outbreak, in 1997), it has slain 60 percent of about 600 people certified as having been infected with it. Predictions of the global toll if H5N1 should turn pandemic reach as high as a billion people.

So why wouldn't a desperate outlaw state—or terrorists—want to weaponize the most dreaded flu strain scientists have ever found?

Because H5N1 would make a wretched weapon.

Influenza in general is an equal-opportunity menace. . . . This would put at great risk anyone trying to assemble a pandemic H5N1 to launch at "target" populations.

To start with, biology is an overrated tool that has rarely brought victory in war. During the American Civil War, for instance, the South employed the timeworn trick of dumping corpses into water supplies needed by its enemies.

The Short History of Biowarfare

The history of biological warfare is an instructively quick read . . . It begins with all of three battles in which aggressors catapulted dead specimens into besieged cities during the Middle Ages; only one surrendered. Then, during the American Revolution, it seems the British tried to infect Yankee rebels with smallpox in Boston and in Canada (where it may have had some effect, following a key defeat) and gave tainted blankets to Native Americans.

Germany tried and failed to sabotage Allied food sources with bacteria during World War I. Japan's Unit 731 committed terrible biological atrocities in China, to little strategic effect, during the 1930s and '40s. With Pentagon support, President Richard M. Nixon scuttled the entire U.S. biowar program, after which the Soviets mounted a huge, expensive effort that accidentally killed almost 70 civilians via an anthrax leak in 1979. An embattled cult in Oregon spread salmonella in salad bars. Japan's murderous Aum Shinrikyo sect collected numerous biological agents but failed to achieve anything with them.

[Iraqi dictator] Saddam Hussein spent a lot of money and effort to emulate the Soviet program, then scuttled it at the [United Nations] UN's behest in 1991. Finally, someone mailed anthrax to prominent Americans shortly after the 9/11 [2001] attacks. The U.S. government blames a top scientist at its biomedical lab at Fort Detrick, Md., who then took his own life.

None of them ever tried to weaponize a flu strain—for good reason. Influenza in general is an equal-opportunity menace, particularly dangerous when a strain is so unfamiliar that humanity lacks immunity to it. This would put at great risk anyone trying to assemble a pandemic H5N1 to launch at "target" populations. Indeed, such an attack would unleash global contagion that would swiftly and inevitably incapacitate an aggressor's own people. Influenza doesn't respect borders.

The worst known flu crisis to date—the Great Pandemic of 1918, thought to have sprung up in Kansas to kill at least 30 million globally—conferred no proven advantage during World War I. Some historians think H1N1 broke the German Army in the midst of its final offensive, but only after ravaging the Allies.

What about terrorists then? Would the doomsday gang Aum Shinrikyo—which in 1995 nerve-gassed Tokyo's subways, killing 13 commuters and injuring around a thousand—have tried to obtain H5N1 and make it transmissible? Aum, one of whose remaining fugitives turned himself in last week, recruited 10,000 Japanese and 30,000 Russians, including many graduates of elite universities. The sect ran sophisticated medical facilities. In addition to nerve agents, Aum stockpiled anthrax and Ebola virus cultures and tried to bomb Tokyo's subways with hydrogen cyanide.

However grisly their effects, Aum's microbial favorites can all be distributed in a controlled fashion. Deep in the African bush, Ebola outbreaks are snuffed out once vectors are identified. Anthrax generally kills those who inhale it but doesn't spread via secondary contact. Aum yearned to unleash biological weapons as a terror tactic, but there's no evidence it embraced any tools whose spread would put its members at risk.

Anyone concerned about bio-terror might contemplate the thousands of newly employed scientists and technicians privy to restricted data and microbial samples.

O.K., suppose a "bad actor" at a high-level government lab were to access and explore, for instance, some research federal authorities are anxious to control. (This is essentially what the FBI [Federal Bureau of Investigation] says led to distribution of anthrax from Fort Detrick, although the bureau's evidential logic has been broadly disputed.)

Benefits Outweigh Risks

Such biomedical labs have multiplied lavishly around the world—particularly in the U.S.—since 9/11. Washington's siting choices raise questions about its commitment to public security. A top-level BSL-4 facility opened in 2009 in Galveston, Tex.—a city flattened in 1900 by a hurricane that a government agency calls "the greatest natural disaster ever to strike the United States." The Plum Island, N.Y., infectious animal disease center is being relocated to a BSL-4 lab under construction in Tornado Alley's Manhattan, Kan.

Indeed, anyone concerned about bio-terror might contemplate the thousands of newly employed scientists and technicians privy to restricted data and microbial samples. Workers at these facilities would undoubtedly rank high on government lists of those who can access restricted research. What makes them safer than academic workers? Will nongovernment scientists have to go through the equivalent of airport sneaker checks to conduct research? In that light, it's significant that the U.S. Centers for Disease Control announced in April [2012] that a team of scientists it sponsored had failed to render H5N1 more transmissible in ferrets. Experts found this comforting. It was evidently misleading.

The public should certainly be concerned about unbridled transport of potentially pandemic flu strains. Rigorous care must be taken lest any escape. But influenza is an extremely dangerous, poorly understood virus. Letting the U.S. government suppress promising scientific work by controlling who can research it and who can assess the results strikes me as the more perilous development.

Eliminating Polio Is a Worthwhile Goal

Matthieu Aikins

Matthieu Aikins is a journalist and writer who is best known for his reporting on the war in Afghanistan.

Only one human disease has been eradicated to date, and it was arguably the most prolific killer in history: smallpox, a virus that brought death to a fifth of its victims and horribly disfigured the rest. Beginning in earnest in 1966, under the leadership of an American epidemiologist from the US Centers for Disease Control, Donald Henderson, WHO [World Health Organization] succeeded in eliminating smallpox by vaccinating more than 80 percent of the world population. But the lengths to which Henderson's team had to go to carry out this feat illustrate just how arduous and risky eradication is. To snuff out the disease in the Eastern Bloc and Southeast Asia, they had to strike up partnerships with Soviet officials at the apex of the Cold War. The campaign enlisted regimes and warring tribes to treat millions of people in 23 smallpox-ridden African countries. At one point, both sides in the shooting war between Nigeria and the Republic of Biafra (a short-lived secessionist state in Nigeria's southeast) agreed to a brief ceasefire so that vaccines could be transported. By the end of 1975, the disease persisted only in the Horn of Africa; it took two years of frantic work to keep it from escaping and to find the final cases. The very last naturally occurring case, a hospital cook in the Somalian town of Merca, was identified and isolated on October 31, 1977. (That man survived and went on to become a vocal leader in Somalia's polio eradication campaign until his death in July of this year [2013].)

The smallpox campaign represented a new kind of success brought about by cooperation on a global scale, one that permanently made the world a better place. Researchers studying smallpox are the only people who have to be vaccinated against it anymore. It's gone. With that success behind them, public-health officials naturally wanted to repeat it with other diseases. After a 17-year campaign, a cattle infection called rinderpest was officially eradicated in 2011. But the struggle to eliminate a second human affliction has proved more difficult than anyone imagined. Yellow fever seemed like a candidate until researchers discovered that the virus also infected primates, which meant eradication couldn't succeed without vaccinating nearly every monkey and ape in the jungle. Similarly, an expensive malaria eradication effort foundered on technical challenges and was abandoned in 1978.

The invisible nature of most infections means that areas thought to have been cleared can flare up again with little warning.

First Smallpox, Then Polio?

Polio, because there's an effective vaccine for it and because it's restricted to humans, also looked like a promising target. By 1988, when WHO and a coalition of governments decided to attack it, the disease had been largely banished from Europe and North America. And yet smallpox, fearsome though it was as a killer, was actually easier to eliminate than polio. This is because—unlike smallpox, which struck its victims with visible pustules and scars—polio is largely invisible, making it far more difficult to track and eliminate.

The poliomyelitis virus has likely been living with humans for millennia. Archaeological excavations of prehistoric burial grounds, as well as paintings in ancient Egyptian monuments, show limb paralysis that is probably the result of polio. The virus, part of the enterovirus genus, is extremely contagious and spreads through two routes—oral-oral, through saliva, or more commonly fecal-oral, like when an infected person's feces contaminate the water supply. In the crowded, unsanitary cities of antiquity and medieval times, this meant that virtually everyone would have been exposed to the virus in childhood. For most people, this wasn't a problem: The virus typically infects only the mucosal tissues of the gastrointestinal system for a few weeks, where the immune system clears it before any harm is done. After that, the infected person would be immune to future infections from the same strain. However, in less than 1 percent of infections, the virus attacks the central nervous system and causes paralysis. Typically this affects just the legs. But in 5 to 10 percent of paralytic cases (that is, 0.05 percent of total infections), polio paralyzes the breathing muscles, meaning that without artificial respiration the patient will suffocate.

All this explains why polio is so difficult to annihilate. For every one person who actually gets sick, nearly 200 are carrying the virus and infecting others. To detect the spread of the disease in Afghanistan as soon as possible, [Ali] Zahed and his colleagues have built a network for reporting suspected cases of polio-related paralysis. Since Afghanistan's public health care system is almost nonexistent in many rural and remote areas, they've recruited all sorts of locals to whom parents are likely to bring a sick child: mullahs, shrine keepers, pharmacists, faith healers, and traveling quacks. They've been given basic training and are paid a reward of about $5 for reporting a confirmed case of paralytic polio. Moreover, advances in rapid genetic sequencing have allowed researchers to chart the path of each infection, showing the complex and often unexpected ways in which polio can travel.

Invisible Virus

Despite such advances, though, the invisible nature of most infections means that areas thought to have been cleared can flare up again with little warning. For example, this year tests of sewage in both Israel and Egypt, which had been deemed polio-free, revealed polio virus that was descended from a strain detected in Pakistan—even though no symptomatic cases have yet been reported in either country. To prevent a return of the virus, population immunity levels need to be kept very high—above 90 percent. And every year, a new cohort of unvaccinated children is born. Unless they are vaccinated, a susceptible population can build, ripe for a return of the virus. In Somalia, polio transmission was stopped in 2007, but fighting between Islamist groups and the Western-backed government in recent years has rendered large areas of the country inaccessible to vaccination programs. The polio campaign watched nervously until finally disaster struck with a new outbreak in May [2013], with nearly 200 cases this year, and some reported in Ethiopia, Kenya, and South Sudan as well. In October, WHO announced that it was investigating a cluster of possible polio cases in Syria, where the conflict has produced more than 2 million refugees.

Although [polio] cases dropped [in Afghanistan] after the fall of the Taliban regime in 2001, an outbreak in 2011 brought 80 new cases and a general sense of emergency.

For all the laurels heaped upon Henderson and the generation of epidemiologists who slew smallpox, eradicating polio may be the hardest initiative that the world public-health community has ever undertaken. Based on the timeline with smallpox, the original vaccination plan in 1988 was that polio would be gone by the turn of the millennium. But in 2000 there were still roughly 700 confirmed cases of polio paralysis worldwide, and the disease remained stubbornly entrenched in Africa and South Asia. Now, 13 years later, the target date has been pushed back to 2018. Reaching that goal depends on the vaccinators who go door to door in the world's most unstable regions, trying to immunize nearly every child.

A Sense of Emergency

In August, I traveled to Jalalabad to observe one of Afghanistan's quarterly National Immunization Days, a three-day span during which the campaign attempts to deliver vaccine to every child under the age of 5. Some 60,000 vaccinators will visit 4.3 million homes and immunize 7.8 million kids, from the scorching deserts of Nimroz Province to the high-altitude valleys of the Wakhan Corridor. Here in Jalalabad, roughly a quarter of the immunization push is overseen by Rana, an unlikely warrior in a region ruled by men with guns: 5 feet tall and slight of build, with a powder-blue burka pulled over her head and high-heeled, glittery sandals peeking out from under its hem. At age 25, Rana will be responsible for managing seven teams of two women apiece, slated to vaccinate 13,952 children in all.

I first meet Rana on the eve of the Immunization Days, at the local campaign headquarters in the Jalalabad hospital. Zahed teases her as she walks by, burka pushed up on her forehead. "Hey, Commander, where are your soldiers?" he asks.

"They'll be ready!" she shoots back. "Tomorrow is a big day."

Because all the Afghan polio cases in 2013 have been reported here in the eastern half of the country, these National Immunization Days have special importance in this region. As with the global campaign writ large, polio here has receded greatly over the past two decades but with serious setbacks along the way: Although cases dropped after the fall of the Taliban regime in 2001, an outbreak in 2011 brought 80 new cases and a general sense of emergency. And so the eradication program—which is government-run but supported financially by WHO and UNICEF [United Nations Children Fund]—ordered a "surge" in Afghanistan. They doubled the international staff and cracked down on underperforming and corrupt officials. This year, the surge has paid a huge dividend, in that the war-torn south of the country, for a long time the greatest problem area, now appears to be free of the virus. It's the inaccessible areas in the east, where Jalalabad is, that are now the main concern. The next day, Rana and her team leaders arrive at the polio headquarters and start packing the navy-blue cylindrical carriers—they look a lot like insulated lunch bags—that they'll take into the field. Each carrier holds roughly a dozen vials of polio vaccine, along with cold packs, applicator nozzles, and, as a bonus, a jar of fruit-flavored deworming tablets. The team leaders load into the waiting vans, and Rana follows behind in a Corolla, chauffeured by her driver. Within the safer confines of the city, all of the vaccination teams are female, which is more effective, since strange men are forbidden from entering domestic spaces.

For the past 10 years, 90 percent of the $300 million annual vaccination budget for WHO in Africa has gone to the eradication of polio—which now afflicts only a few hundred people per year.

Rana's father is elderly, and she doesn't have any brothers, so it has fallen to her, as the oldest daughter, to be the main breadwinner in the family. She graduated from teacher's college but has been unable to find a full-time job in a school. In the conservative segments of Afghan society—which describes all but a tiny slice of the elite and the urban upper-middle class—it's considered a bit disreputable for a woman to work outside the home, especially in a job that involves going door-to-door. So Rana and her colleagues are mostly here out of financial necessity. Not that they get paid much—the vaccinators earn the equivalent of $3.50 a day, whereas a male laborer makes at least $6. Even as a supervisor, Rana earns only about $4 a day.

She heads out to check on a team in a suburb of the city. Eventually we spot them standing near a gaudy mansion the locals have dubbed the White House. Next door lies a set of interconnected mud hovels bordering a sewage ditch that bubbles slowly, its surface covered in ropes of black algae and crowded with flies. Three ducks float in the ditch, snuffling at the scum. Further down, shrieking children scramble barefoot through the mud and splash in the water. It's easy to see how the fecal-oral route works here. As Rana and her team go into the mud dwellings, an older man comes out and stands beside me on the edge of the ditch. His name is Ali Mohammed, and his family lives in just one of the single-room hovels. He has a long black beard, and he twists it as he talks. Twenty years ago, he says, he came from a rural mountain village in neighboring Kunar Province, looking to escape the chaos and violence of the civil war that had been sparked by the defeat of the Soviets. Now he works as a cook, earning about $80 a month, and rents the hovel. At 40, he is old enough to remember the smallpox eradication campaigns and approves of the polio one. "Allah Almighty provides us help, but this is his means," he says.

Economics of Eradication

A health worker marks a door in the university district to show residents have been vaccinated The Eradication campaigns follow a necessary logic. As the smallpox precedent shows, once you have beaten back a disease to just a few hundred cases, they will almost by definition be concentrated in places where there's some barrier—geographical, cultural, political—to easy vaccination. In general, each marginal case will cost more, and will consume more time and effort and labor, than the one before it. This hockey-stick curve was true of smallpox, and it's proving to be true of polio.

Robert Steinglass, who directs an immunization project funded by the Bill & Melinda Gates Foundation, points out that for the past 10 years, 90 percent of the $300 million annual vaccination budget for WHO in Africa has gone to the eradication of polio—which now afflicts only a few hundred people per year. More than $1 billion is spent on the polio campaign each year. By comparison, the Global Fund to Fight AIDS, Tuberculosis, and Malaria—diseases that kill approximately 3.2 million people each year—is seeking $15 billion in funding through 2016.

Is the polio campaign worth it? I pose this question to Steven Rosenthal, an epidemiologist at the CDC [Centers for Disease Control and Prevention] who is visiting Jalalabad to observe the National Immunization Days. He's been working on polio since 1995, when the CDC sent him to Indonesia to work on the campaign there. Though Indonesia ended transmission by 2006, the reality that the campaign would be a long haul began to weigh on Rosenthal then, especially when faced with the major setbacks in South Asia and Africa. "At the time," he recalls, "I worried that the problems were too complex to ever be solved." But, he goes on, the teams in these regions—particularly in India, which eliminated transmission in 2011, an enormous success story by any standard—learned how to solve the worst of their problems, which centered around vaccinating an extremely dense and impoverished population by means of a corrupt and barely functioning health care system. The key was getting above that 90 percent immunity threshold, and they did it. In Rosenthal's mind, that was the turning point in the campaign, and recent setbacks—like the one in Somalia—have been relatively minor by comparison.

Against critics who blanch at the cost of eradication, Rosenthal counters that the polio campaign is paying dividends throughout the global health system. In Afghanistan, as elsewhere, the initiative is training a generation of health care workers like Rana in modern, goal-oriented public health practices: ... In Indonesia, Rosenthal points out, "the polio lab network we built wound up forming the backbone for their measles campaign. Working on the polio campaign changed the way their public health officials work."

Moreover, the math of cost-benefit analyses runs aground when it comes to eradication campaigns, because the benefits, in theory, are infinite. That is: No one will ever die from—or spend a dime on vaccinating against—smallpox for the remainder of human history, barring a disaster involving one of the few lingering military stockpiles. According to a 2010 study, polio eradication would generate $40 billion to $50 billion in net benefits by 2035. Looking at a long enough timescale, the eradication of polio could someday be seen as positively cheap.

Eliminating Polio May Be Impossible

Daniel Stolte

Daniel Stolte is a writer at UA News.

Efforts at eradicating diseases may be doomed because of a mismatch between the ways humans structure the world and the ways pathogens move through the world, a team of University of Arizona geography experts writes in a commentary published in *The Lancet Infectious Diseases*, one of the world's most prestigious medical journals.

Missed Deadline

"The 2013 deadline for the worldwide goal to eradicate polio has come and gone, with a new endgame set for 2018," the authors note. They are Vincent Del Casino, Melinda Butterworth and Georgia Davis, all in the UA [University of Arizona] School of Geography and Development.

In 1988, the 41st World Health Assembly adopted a resolution for the worldwide eradication of polio. It marked the launch of the Global Polio Eradication Initiative, spearheaded by national governments, the World Health Organization, Rotary International, the U.S. Centers for Disease Control and Prevention and UNICEF [United Nations Children's Fund] with support from key partners including the Bill and Melinda Gates Foundation.

The commentary uses the deadline, and a resurfacing of the virus, as a springboard to addresses the big picture of how to understand and manage infectious diseases in a complex and changing world. The timing of the commentary coincides with a blow to immunization efforts, including violent acts against health workers in Pakistan and Nigeria, where rumors persist that the polio vaccine is part of a Western plot.

"If you put all your energy into eradication, you miss opportunities for mitigation and management," said Del Casino, professor of geography and development and vice provost for digital learning and student engagement. "We hope to suggest that we can use polio as an entry point to a larger conversation about the spread of viruses more generally."

One of the biggest challenges in ridding the world of polio is a mismatch in the way humans perceive and structure the world and the ways viruses . . . move through the world.

Unlike smallpox, poliomyelitis—a debilitating disease affecting the nervous system and causing permanent paralysis—has never been completely eradicated, Del Casino said.

"Smallpox eradication is rather unique and took a massive global effort, an incredibly expensive and coordinated effort that may not be possible with other infectious diseases."

According to the authors, one of the biggest challenges in ridding the world of polio is a mismatch in the way humans perceive and structure the world and the ways viruses—and, by extension, other pathogens—move through the world.

How the Virus Sees the World

"The ways we believe the world is structured clash with the structure of the world that is relevant to the virus," Del Casino explained. "If we were to scale down our focus from the world of humans to the world of viruses, we'd end up in a different place in how we imagine the world and we'd start to think differently. Polioviruses don't need or rely on our view of the world. Their existence is based on human bodies and how to move from one to the next."

"In our society, we have a tendency to make sense of the world by organizing it into boxes," said Davis, a doctoral candidate in the School of Geography and Development. "We think certain pathogens occur here, but not there, and they get from this host to that host, and this is how they do it. But in reality, our attempt to understand the world by ordering it in certain ways may actually preclude us from really understanding it."

"Put another way," the authors write, "polioviruses maintain themselves by seeping through the boundaries—real or imagined—we use to contain them. In view of this, we need a more cautious approach to our thinking, and might need to reduce our expectations of global eradication efforts."

With Lyme, for instance, reporting happens on a county level, Davis said. On some maps, it appears that Lyme is endemic in one county but almost nonexistent just across the county border. "It's the same for dengue fever," said Butterworth, also a doctoral candidate in the School of Geography and Development, who researches the mosquito-borne disease. "We're seeing a global resurgence of the virus, including several recent outbreaks in the U.S. Yet dengue is mostly thought of as a 'tropical disease,' so the diagnosis isn't always made."

"The issue of accurate testing and reporting of infectious diseases is a classic concern in health and medical science," Butterworth added. "But it matters for geography too, because it influences what our maps of disease distributions look like. Those maps influence how we understand where diseases are, and how we test for and monitor their spread."

The picture gets even more complicated in light of conflicts between people or entire nations, climate change and health care disparities.

"Climate and environmental changes alter the habitats of pathogens and vectors in ways we're still trying to understand," Butterworth said.

"Let's say a particular nation has vaccination programs, but a neighboring country doesn't, and yet another has them but can't enforce them uniformly," Davis explained. "Add migration to the mix and you can see how this creates holes for pathogens to move through and escape our ability to map them, let alone eradicate them."

The number of new polio cases has dropped dramatically, from 716 in 2011 to 223 in 2013, but more cases are cropping up. "What is interesting is that, since 2013, which saw tensions in Somalia, the crisis in Syria, and a deteriorating situation in Afghanistan, there has been a creeping increase in cases," Del Casino said. "There almost was a chance to contain the virus, but it has become very difficult to contain those spaces, because viruses move faster than that."

Organizations to Contact

The editors have compiled the following list of organizations concerned with the issues debated in this book. The descriptions are derived from materials provided by the organizations. All have publications or information available for interested readers. The list was compiled on the date of publication of the present volume; names, addresses, phone and fax numbers, and e-mail and Internet addresses may change. Be aware that many organizations take several weeks or longer to respond to inquiries, so allow as much time as possible.

AVERT
4 Brighton Rd., Horsham, West Sussex   RF13 5BA
  UK
+44 (0)1403 210202.
e-mail: info@avert.org
website: www.avert.org

The international AIDS charity AVERT works to reduce the number and impact of HIV/AIDS infections globally through education and promotion of positive, proactive treatment of the disease. Many of the organization's projects focus on Africa and India, with an emphasis on prevention as well as aid for those already impacted by AIDS. AVERT's website offers regional summaries of the AIDS epidemic as well as more detailed, specific reports about the prevalence of the disease within particular countries such as South Africa, Malawi, and Uganda. The website also offers resources targeted at gay men and women, such as the booklet *Young Gay Men Talking*.

Centers for Disease Control and Prevention (CDC)
1600 Clifton Rd., Atlanta, GA   30333
(404) 639-3534 • fax: (800) 311-3435
website: www.cdc.gov

The Centers for Disease Control and Prevention, founded in 1946, was originally charged with the task of finding methods to control malaria. Since its inception, the agency's mission has broadened, but there is still a focus on preventing and managing both communicable and noncommunicable diseases. The CDC offers guidelines for professionals and the general public on how to behave in order to slow or prevent the spread of infectious disease. The organization also provides extensive research on the ways in which vaccinations are administered, the possibility of future pandemics, and new methods to prevent pandemics. Two topical publications by the CDC are *Emerging Infectious Diseases Journal* and *Preventing Chronic Disease Journal*.

Childhood Influenza Immunization Coalition (CIIC)
90 Fifth Ave., Suite 800, New York, NY   10011-2052
(212) 886-2277
e-mail: CIIC@nfid.org
website: www.preventchildhoodinfluenza.org

The Childhood Influenza Immunization Coalition was established by the National Foundation for Infectious Diseases (NFID) to protect infants, children, and adolescents from influenza by communicating the need to make influenza immunization a national health priority and by seeking to improve the low influenza immunization rates among children. Its members represent twenty-five of the nation's leading public health, medical, patient, and parent groups. The group's website includes information for the media, healthcare professionals, and the public, including the report *Improving Childhood Influenza Immunization Rates to Protect Our Nation's Children*.

Infectious Diseases Society of America (IDSA)
66 Canal Center Plaza, Suite 600, Alexandria, VA   22314
(703) 299-0200 • fax: (703) 299-0204
e-mail: info@idsociety.org
website: www.idsociety.org

The Infectious Diseases Society of America is an organization of healthcare and scientific professionals concerned with the prevention and treatment of infectious diseases. The society provides research suggesting how to provide the best care for individuals with communicable diseases. IDSA also works as an advocacy group promoting sound public policy on infectious diseases. IDSA's website includes many resources, articles, and fact pages. In addition to the *IDSA News*, the organization publishes the journals *Clinical Infectious Diseases* and the *Journal of Infectious Diseases*.

National Vaccine Information Center (NVIC)
204 Mill St., Suite B1, Vienna, VA   22180
(703) 938-0342 • fax: (703) 938-5768
website: www.nvic.org

The National Vaccine Information Center, a national, nonprofit educational organization, is the oldest and largest consumer organization advocating the institution of vaccine safety and informed consent protections in the mass vaccination system. It is dedicated to the prevention of vaccine injuries and deaths through public education. As an independent clearinghouse for information on diseases and vaccines, NVIC does not promote the use of vaccines and does not advise against the use of vaccines; it supports the availability of all preventive healthcare options and the right of consumers to make educated, voluntary healthcare choices. NVIC publishes a free newsletter, and its website includes fact sheets and articles.

United Nations Children's Fund (UNICEF)
125 Maiden Lane, New York, NY   10038
(212) 326-7000 • fax: (212) 887-7465
website: www.unicef.org

The United Nations Children's Fund works to help build a world where the rights of every child are realized. UNICEF works to prevent the spread of infectious viruses among young people and helps children and families affected by HIV/AIDS to live their lives with dignity. UNICEF publishes numerous briefing papers, available at its website.

US Agency for International Development (USAID)

Information Center, Ronald Reagan Building
Washington, DC   20523-1000
(202) 712-4810 • fax: (202) 216-3524
website: www.usaid.gov

The US Agency for International Development is an international aid organization of the US government. Program goals include disaster relief, aid for countries attempting to end poverty, and promotion of democratic reform. One important facet addressed in order to achieve these goals is disease prevention and management. USAID provides programs and funding to aid in the fight against these pandemics worldwide. USAID's monthly news publication, *Frontlines*, is published in print and electronically.

US Department of Health and Human Services (HHS)

200 Independence Ave. SW, Washington, DC   20201
(202) 691-0257 • fax: (877) 696-6775
website: www.hhs.gov

The Department of Health and Human Services is the US government agency that concentrates on the public's health and wellbeing. It is the parent agency of other government health organizations such as the Centers for Disease Control and Prevention and the National Institutes of Health. Among the agency's many services, disease prevention and immunization are a top priority. HHS manages many services dedicated not only to researching new options to combat disease but also to create informative programs for the public. The HHS website includes fact sheets, news reports, transcripts of congressional testimony, and more.

Vaccine Education Center at the Children's Hospital of Philadelphia

The Children's Hospital of Philadelphia
Philadelphia, PA   19104
website: http://vec.chop.edu/service/vaccine-education-center

The Children's Hospital of Philadelphia is one of the leading pediatric hospitals and research facilities in the world. Its Vaccine Education Center webpage contains detailed information about each available vaccine, plus the answers to general questions about vaccination. The site includes instructions on how to receive the "Parents Pack Monthly Newsletter" dealing with vaccination issues.

World Health Organization (WHO)

Avenue Appia 20, 1211, Geneva   27
  Switzerland
+ 41 22 791 21 11 • fax: + 41 22 791 31 11
website: www.who.int

The World Health Organization is an agency of the United Nations formed in 1948 with the goal of creating and ensuring a world where all people can live with high levels of both mental and physical health. The organization researches and endorses different methods of combating the spread of diseases. WHO publishes the *Bulletin of the World Health Organization*, which is available online, as well as the *Pan American Journal of Public Health*. Within WHO, the Pan American Health Organization is the regional office that covers the United States.

Bibliography

Books

Dorothy H. Crawford	*Virus Hunt: The Search for the Origin of HIV*. New York: Oxford University Press, 2013.
Dorothy H. Crawford	*Viruses: A Very Short Introduction*. New York: Oxford University Press, 2011.
Hung Y. Fan, Ross F. Conner, and Luis P. Villarreal	*AIDS: Science and Society*, 7th ed. Sudbury, MA: Jones & Bartlett Learning, 2013.
Michael Greger	*Bird Flu: A Virus of Our Own Hatching*. New York: Lantern Books, 2006.
D.A. Henderson	*Smallpox: The Death of a Disease—The Inside Story of Eradicating a Worldwide Killer*. Amherst, NY: Prometheus Books, 2009.
Nathalia Holt	*Cured: How the Berlin Patients Defeated HIV and Forever Changed Science*. New York: Plume, 2014.
Gina Kolata	*Flu: The Story of the Great Influenza Pandemic of 1918 and the Search for the Virus That Caused It*. New York: Touchstone, 2001.

Seth Mnookin   *The Panic Virus: The True Story
                      Behind the Vaccine-Autism
                      Controversy.* New York: Simon &
                      Schuster, 2012.

William Muraskin *Polio Eradication and Its Discontents:
                      A Historian's Journey Through an
                      International Public Health (Un)Civil
                      War.* Telangana, India: Orient
                      Blackswan, 2012.

Paul A. Offit   *Deadly Choices: How the Anti-Vaccine
                      Movement Threatens Us All.* New
                      York: Basic Books, 2012.

Richard Preston   *The Hot Zone: The Terrifying True
                      Story of the Origins of the Ebola
                      Virus.* New York: Anchor, 1995.

David Quammen   *The Chimp and the River: How AIDS
                      Emerged from an African Forest.* New
                      York: W.W. Norton, 2015.

David Quammen   *Ebola: The Natural and Human
                      History of a Deadly Virus.* New York:
                      W.W. Norton, 2014.

Aviva Jill Romm   *Vaccinations, a Thoughtful Parent's
                      Guide: How to Make Safe, Sensible
                      Decisions About the Risks, Benefits,
                      and Alternatives.* Rochester, VT:
                      Healing Arts Press, 2010.

Gareth Williams   *Angel of Death: The Story of
                      Smallpox.* London, United Kingdom:
                      Palgrave Macmillan, 2011.

Periodicals and Internet Resources

James Ball	"Concerned About Ebola? You're Worrying About the Wrong Disease," *Guardian*, August 5, 2014.
BBC	"Ebola: The Race for Drugs and Vaccines," February 24, 2015. www.bbc.com.
Jessica Berman	"Researchers Think Synthetic Vaccine Could Eliminate Polio," Voice of America, February 16, 2015. www.voanews.com.
Lenny Bernstein	"Why You're Not Going to Get Ebola in the U.S.," *Washington Post*, August 1, 2014.
Amy Brittain	"The Search for an Ebola Cure Is Gearing Up—But There May Be Too Few Patients," *Washington Post*, February 10, 2014.
Maggie Fox	"Bird Flu Mutating in China, Threatens Pandemic," NBC News, March 11, 2015. www.nbcnews.com.
Amanda Gardner	"HIV: Is a Cure in Reach?" WebMD, n.d. www.webmd.com.
Benjamin Hale	"The Most Terrifying Thing About Ebola," *Slate*, September 19, 2014. www.slate.com.
Henry J. Kaiser Family Foundation	"Black Americans and HIV/AIDS," April 25, 2014. www.kff.org.

Karen Kaplan   "Vaccine Refusal Helped Fuel
                    Disneyland Measles Outbreak, Study
                    Says," *Los Angeles Times*, March 16,
                    2015.

Erik Lacitis   "Vashon Parents Try to Get Along
                    Despite Deep Divide over
                    Vaccination," *Seattle Times*, March 17,
                    2015.

Donald G.   "U.S. Push for Abstinence in Africa Is
McNeil Jr.   Seen as Failure Against H.I.V.," *New
                    York Times*, February 26, 2015.

Steven Novella   "Should Vaccines Be Compulsory?,"
                    Science-Based Medicine, June 3,
                    2009. www.sciencebasedmedicine.org.

Tom Odula   "International Health Groups Say
                    AIDS No. 1 Killer of Adolescents in
                    Africa and 2nd Globally," *U.S. News
                    & World Report*, February 17, 2015.

Dileep Kumar   "Failure of Polio Eradication in
Rohra   Conflict Areas: Another Perspective,"
                    British Medical Journal, May 6, 2014.

Kathleen Sebelius   "Why We Still Need Smallpox," *New
                    York Times*, April 25, 2011.

Jeffrey A. Singer   "Vaccination and Free Will," Cato
                    Institute, April 2014. www.cato.org.

Rob Stein   "Should Last Remaining Known
                    Smallpox Virus Die?" *Washington
                    Post*, March 8, 2011.

Ira Straus   "Mandatory Vaccination Is
                      Conservative," *National Review*,
                      February 4, 2015.

Marisa Taylor   "Antiretroviral Drug Greatly Reduces
                      HIV Transmission Risk, New Study
                      Says," Aljazeera America, February
                      25, 2015. www.america.aljazeera.com.

Index

A

B

NewLink Genetics, 58
The New York Times (newspaper),
21, 44
Nigeria, 27, 34, 38, 41, 118, 182,
192
nongovernmental organizations
(NGOs), 121
nonmedical exemptions for vac-
cines, 78–81
Norwegian Knowledge Centre for
the Health Services, 103
Novavax, 59
Nyangoma, Edith N., 89–94
Nyhan, Brendan, 73, 85–88

O

Obama, Barack
AIDS remarks by, 116
appointment of coordinator
for Ebola, 36
Ebola treatment units, 40, 49
overview, 29, 30–33, 48
Operation United Assistance, 31
oral adenovirus platform, 59

P

Pakistan, 102, 185, 192
Patient Safety Authority, 35
Paul Allen Family Foundation, 33
Pearson, Rachel, 108–112
Pediatrics journal, 84
Pence, Mike, 114–115
People Who Inject Drugs (PWID),
130–131
personal-belief exemptions to vac-
cines, 77
pertussis threat, 56, 80
Planned Parenthood, 114

polio virus
Afghanistan, 184, 186–188
economics of eradication,
188–190
elimination deadlines, 191–
192
elimination difficulties, 191–
194
elimination goals, 182–190
invisible nature of, 184–186
overview, 182–183
polymerase chain reaction (PCR),
90, 92
post-exposure prophylaxis, 127
post-exposure vaccination, 91
Power, Samantha, 50
President's Emergency Plan for
AIDS Relief (PEPFAR) initiative,
118, 139
prevent the mother-to-child transmission of HIV (PMTCT), 131
Price, Jenna, 65–66
Public Health Agency of Canada,
58
public health failure over Ebola
virus, 39–41
public health threats in Texas,
55–57

Q

quarantines, 41, 52, 55, 99, 150

R

rabies, 20–23
Raoult, Didier, 135
recombinant influenza candidate,
59
recombinant rabies vaccine, 59